OCS Report
MMS 2007-021

I0411756

# Deepwater Gulf of Mexico 2007: Interim Report of 2006 Highlights

Authors

Robert H. Peterson
G. Ed Richardson
Christy M. Bohannon
Eric G. Kazanis
Tara M. Montgomery
Lesley D. Nixon
Mike P. Gravois
Gregory D. Klocek

**U.S. Department of the Interior**
Minerals Management Service
Gulf of Mexico OCS Region

New Orleans
May 2007

# PREFACE

This is the seventh publication that the Minerals Management Service (MMS) has released chronicling the levels of deepwater exploration, development, and production activities in the Gulf of Mexico (GOM).

This past year has seen significant advances in exploration and development. In 2006, twelve new deepwater discoveries were announced by industry as a result of ambitious exploration programs. These discoveries are estimated to add approximately 1.3 billion barrels of oil equivalent (BOE) to the GOM reserves base. Some of these discoveries were located in the new Lower Tertiary trend, where large oil and gas volumes have been encountered, but have only been lightly tested. The first sustained well test in the trend, the Jack 2 well, occurred last year and its results are being carefully analyzed. Data from this test were highly publicized and are very encouraging; however, many questions remain to be answered before it is determined whether the hydrocarbon resources throughout the trend will be economically recoverable. Over the next few years, it is anticipated that one or more fields will be producing from this large deepwater trend.

Deepwater production has continued to be a very important part of the total GOM production, providing 70 percent of the oil and 40 percent of the gas in the region. Since the year 2000, more oil has been produced in the deepwater areas of the GOM than from shallower waters. Nineteen of the 20 highest producing blocks in the GOM were in the deepwater area.

Several other noteworthy events occurred in 2006. The passage of the Gulf of Mexico Energy Security Act of 2006 late last year will open two new areas in the deepwater GOM to leasing activities; it placed leasing moratoria on other areas; and it increases the distribution of offshore oil and gas revenues to coastal producing states. New planning area/sale boundaries were established, and the royalty rate for deepwater leases was increased to 16.7 percent (up from 12.5%).

The oil and gas industry is "pushing the envelope" of technology in drilling wells in water depths of over 10,000 feet (ft) (3,048 meters (m)); and with well depths in excess of 30,000 ft (9,144 m), many are under high temperature and high pressure conditions. State-of-the-art technologies must be developed and implemented. Last year, MMS approved 30 new technologies for use in the deepwater GOM. To ensure safe drilling and production operations in the GOM, MMS continues to work with the American Petroleum Institute (API) to write and update standards for offshore activities.

The MMS plays a critical role in the sound development of energy resources in the deepwater GOM. By ensuring the receipt of fair market value for the sale of leases, encouraging conservation, evaluating and approving new technology, and regulating the drilling and production of fields in ever deepening water depths, MMS is a responsible steward of U.S. offshore resources.

Lars Herbst
Acting Regional Director
Minerals Management Service

# TABLE OF CONTENTS

# FIGURES

# TABLES

# ABBREVIATIONS AND ACRONYMS

| | |
|---|---|
| ac | acres |
| AC | Alaminos Canyon |
| AL | Alabama |
| API | American Petroleum Institute |
| AT | Atwater Valley |
| ATB | articulated tug barge |
| bbl | barrel |
| BBOE | billion barrels of oil equivalent |
| Bcf | billion cubic feet |
| Bcfpd | billion cubic feet per day |
| BOE | barrels of oil equivalent |
| BP | British Petroleum |
| Call/NOI | Call for Information and Nominations/Notice of Intent |
| CASE | Climate and Simulation of Eddies |
| cfpd | cubic feet per day |
| CFR | Code of Federal Regulations |
| CGOM | Central Gulf of Mexico |
| CICESE | Centro de Investigación Científica y de Educación Superior de Ensenada |
| CID | Conservation Information Document |
| CPA | Central Planning Area |
| DC | DeSoto Canyon |
| DOCD | Development Operations Coordination Document |
| DWOP | Deep Water Operations Plan |
| DWRRA | Deep Water Royalty Relief Act |
| EA | environmental assessment |
| EB | East Breaks |
| EGOM | Eastern Gulf of Mexico |
| EIA | Energy Information Administration |
| EIS | environmental impact statement |
| EJIP | Eddy Joint Industry Project |
| EP | Exploration Plan |
| EPA | Eastern Planning Area |
| EW | Ewing Bank |
| FL | Florida |
| FPS | floating production system |
| FPSO | floating production, storage, and offloading |
| FPU | floating production unit |

| | |
|---|---|
| FSHR | free-standing hybrid risers |
| ft | feet |
| GB | Garden Banks |
| GC | Green Canyon |
| GOM | Gulf of Mexico |
| GOMESA | Gulf of Mexico Energy Security Act of 2006 |
| HEAT | Hurricane Evacuation and Assessment Team |
| HIPPS | high integrity pressure protection system |
| ITB | integrated tug barge |
| KC | Keathley Canyon |
| km | kilometers |
| kn | knots |
| LA | Louisiana |
| LL | Lloyd Ridge |
| LSU | Louisiana State University |
| LWCF | Land and Water Conservation Fund |
| m | meters |
| Mbopd | thousand barrels of oil per day |
| MC | Mississippi Canyon |
| Mcf | thousand cubic feet |
| Mcfg | thousand cubic feet of gas |
| mi | miles |
| MMbbl | million barrels |
| MMcfpd | million cubic feet per day |
| MMS | Minerals Management Service |
| MODU | mobile offshore drilling unit |
| MS | Mississippi |
| MTLP | mini-tension-leg platform |
| NDBC | National Data Buoy Center |
| NEPA | National Environmental Policy Act |
| NTL | Notice to Lessees and Operators |
| OCS | Offshore Continental Shelf |
| PDQ | production, drilling, and quarters |
| PEA | programmatic environmental assessment |
| PIES | inverted echo sounder with pressure |
| RP | recommended practices |

| | | | |
|---|---|---|---|
| SBS | separation and boosting system | TX | Texas |
| SEBCEP | Sigsbee Escarpment Bottom Current Enhancement Project | U.S. | United States |
| | | USDOE | United States Department of Energy |
| SEIS | supplemental environmental impact statement | USDOI | United States Department of the Interior |
| SITP | shut-in tubing pressure | VK | Viosca Knoll |
| ST | South Timbalier | WGOM | Western Gulf of Mexico |
| TLP | tension-leg platform | WR | Walker Ridge |

# INTRODUCTION

The Deepwater Gulf of Mexico 2007 report is a condensed and updated edition of the biennial deepwater report published by MMS. The 2007 report provides an up-to-date review of activities in the deepwater GOM, including highlights from 2006.

With the passage of the Gulf of Mexico Energy Security Act of 2006, new areas will be opened for leasing in the Central and Eastern Planning Areas. The MMS also altered the boundaries for all three planning areas in the GOM. These new boundaries will go into effect on July 1, 2007, concurrently with the new 5-Year Program (2007-2012), which establishes the offshore lease sales for the Nation.

Exploration activity was strong again in the deepwater GOM. Deepwater exploratory drilling increased in 2006 with 101 wells drilled, compared with 93 wells drilled in 2005. The number of exploratory wells drilled in greater than 5,000 ft (1,524 m) of water rose from 25 in 2005 to 35 in 2006. Recent exploration efforts resulted in the announcement of 12 new deepwater field discoveries (see table 1). Four of these discoveries were drilled in water depths greater than 5,000 ft (1,524 m).

Significant milestones have also occurred in deepwater development activity. In addition to first production from 10 new deepwater fields, MMS approved 30 new technology applications. These technology advancements include a High Integrity Pressure Protection System (HIPPS), a conceptual plan for a Floating Production, Storage, and Offloading (FPSO) vessel, and the use of subsea boosting and processing equipment. The MMS and the oil and gas industry have continued to work together to revise and improve many of the API documents that serve as recommended practices to guide operational activities.

**This report is divided into five sections.**

The **Background** section

- explains administrative boundary changes,

- highlights exploration activity in the Lower Tertiary trend, and

- provides information on current deepwater GOM discoveries.

The **Leasing and Environment** section

- depicts leasing activities and trends,

- explains future leasing activities, including anticipated lease expirations, and

- discusses regulatory and environmental issues.

The **Drilling and Development** section

- provides information on operational plans,

- deepwater drilling activities,

- approval of new technologies, and

- deepwater development systems.

1

The **Reserves and Production** section

- explains large, new discovered volumes in 2006,
- shows production rates and trends,
- explains the importance of the deepwater areas to GOM production, and
- discusses production recovery from Hurricanes Katrina and Rita.

The **Summary and Conclusions** section

- highlights activities that occurred in 2006,
- shows the impact of oil and gas prices on lease activities,
- explains drilling to production lag times, and
- describes difficulties in evaluating deepwater leases before their lease terms expire.

See table 1 below for a listing of the 2006 announced deepwater discoveries in the GOM.

Table 1
2006 Announced Deepwater Discoveries in the Gulf of Mexico

| Prospect | Operator | Area/Block | Water Depth* (ft) |
|---|---|---|---|
| Gotcha | TOTAL E&P USA | Alaminos Canyon 856 | 7,600 |
| Mission Deep | Anadarko | Green Canyon 955 | 7,300 |
| Kaskida | BP | Keathley Canyon 292 | 5,860 |
| Thunder Bird | Murphy | Mississippi Canyon 819 | 5,673 |
| Caesar | Anadarko | Green Canyon 683 | 4,457 |
| Friesian | Shell | Green Canyon 599 | 3,800 |
| Claymore | Anadarko | Atwater Valley 140 | 3,700 |
| Pony | Hess Corporation | Green Canyon 468 | 3,440 |
| Raton | Noble Energy | Mississippi Canyon 248 | 3,400 |
| Redrock | Noble Energy | Mississippi Canyon 204 | 3,334 |
| Ringo | Nexen | Mississippi Canyon 546 | 2,500 |
| Longhorn North | Eni | Mississippi Canyon 502 | 2,330 |

* Water depths are approximate.

# BACKGROUND

## DEFINITIONS

For purposes of this report, deepwater is defined as water depths greater than or equal to 1,000 ft (305 m). More detailed definitions may be found in the annual *Estimated Oil and Gas Reserves, Gulf of Mexico, December 31, 2003* report (Crawford et al., 2006).

This 2007 report refers to deepwater developments by field names and operator-designated project names. Appendix A, Development Systems of Productive Deepwater GOM Projects, provides locations and additional information regarding these fields and projects. All production volumes and rates reflect data through December 2005, unless otherwise noted.

## CHANGE IN ADMINISTRATIVE BOUNDARIES (SALE BOUNDARIES)

On January 3, 2006, MMS published a notice in the *Federal Register* (2006; 71 FR 1) announcing the setting of Federal Outer Continental Shelf (OCS) offshore administrative boundaries beyond State submerged lands for planning, coordination, and administrative purposes. As a result, the GOM planning area boundaries have been moved to correspond to the new administrative lines. The planning area boundary change will take effect with the 2007-2012 5-Year Program on July 1, 2007. Lease Sales for the 2007-2012 5-Year Program are based on these new administrative boundaries. More information on how the administrative boundaries were developed can be found on the MMS's Internet website at http://www.mms.gov/ld/AdminBoundaries.htm. Figures 1 and 2 show the changes in the planning area boundaries. The new planning area boundaries will appear on all pertinent maps in this report; however, historic data will refer to the old planning area boundaries.

## EXPANDING FRONTIER

At the end of 2006, there were 122 producing projects in the GOM's deepwater areas, up from 118 producing projects as of March 2006. Over the last 15 years, there has been an expansion in many phases of deepwater activity. There are approximately 7,855 active leases in the Gulf of Mexico OCS, 54 percent of which are in deepwater. (Note that lease status may change daily, so the current number of active leases is an approximation.) Contrast this to approximately 5,600 active GOM leases in 1992, only 27 percent of which were in deepwater. On average, there were 30 rigs drilling in deepwater in 2006, compared with only 3 rigs in 1992.

## EXPLORATION ACTIVITY

Exploration drilling in the deepwater GOM has found oil and gas resources totaling more than 5 BBOE since 2002, double the amount reported in the 2005 Deepwater Interim Report (French et al., 2005). Recent discoveries in new deepwater plays continue to expand the exploration potential of the GOM. Several recently announced deepwater discoveries encountered large potential reservoirs in sands of Lower Tertiary age (Oligocene, Eocene, and Paleocene).

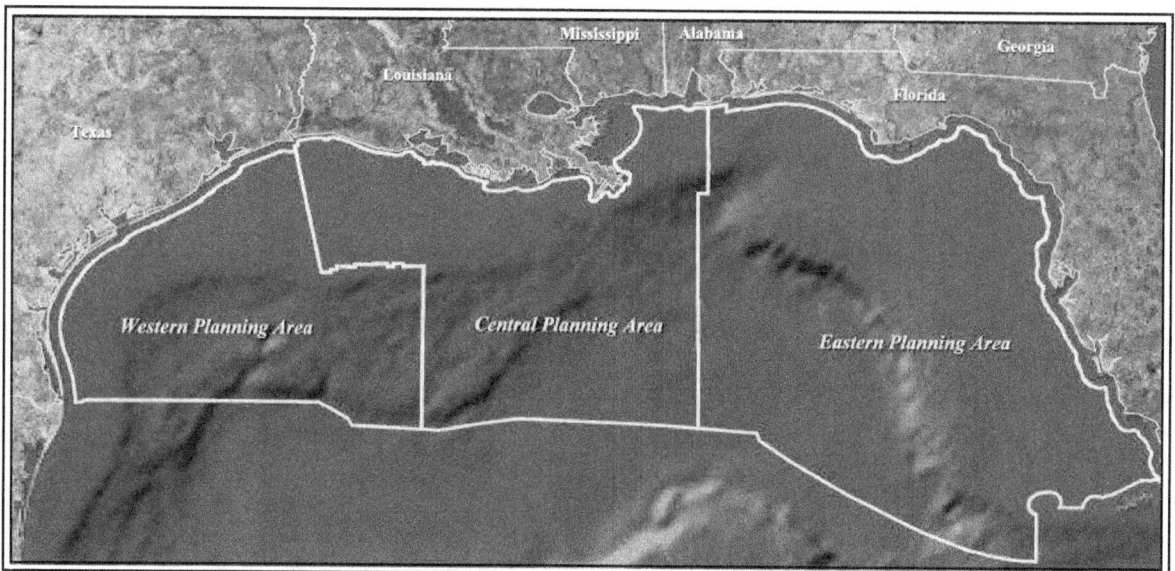

Figure 1. Current planning areas in the Gulf of Mexico.

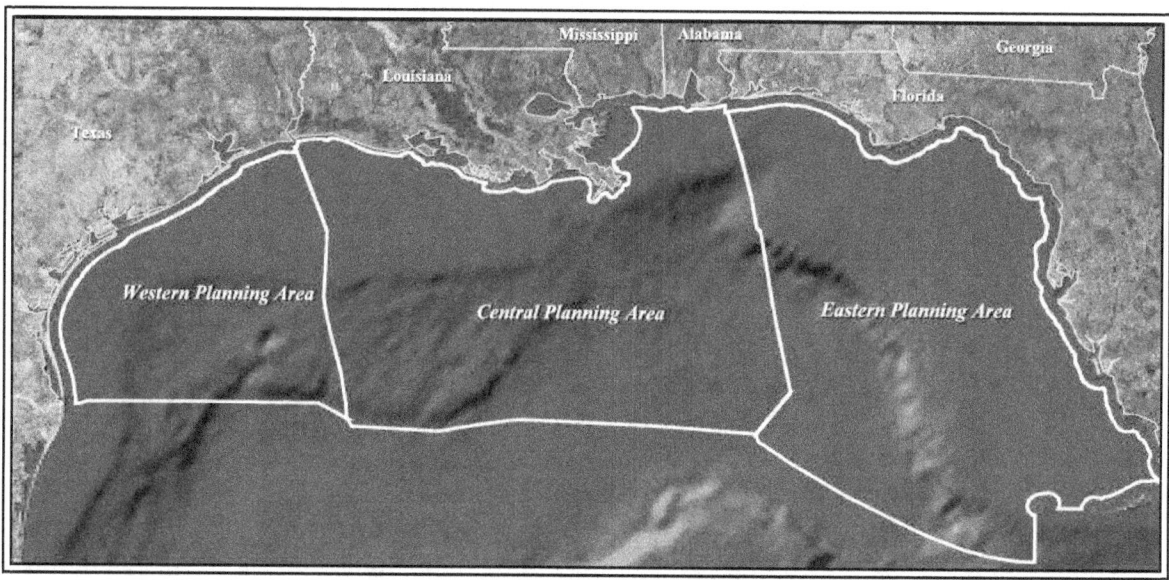

Figure 2. New planning areas in the Gulf of Mexico.

This older portion of the Tertiary section has been lightly tested in the GOM, and the discovery of reservoirs of this geologic age has opened wide areas of the GOM to further exploration. The stratigraphic section in figure 3 shows that there are few current proved reserves in the Lower Tertiary trend, but newly announced discoveries (with an estimated potential 1.3 billion barrels of producible hydrocarbons) may represent a nearly 10 percent addition to total GOM oil and gas volumes.

| System | Time (mya) | Series | Percent of Total Proved Reserves | Discovered BOE All Water Depths | Discovered BOE Water Depths >1,000 ft |
|---|---|---|---|---|---|
| Tertiary | Upper | 24 | Miocene - Pleistocene | 99% | 88% (12.7 BBOE) | 88% (9.2 BBOE) |
| | Lower | 65 | Paleocene  Eocene  Oligocene | — | 9% (1.3 BBOE) | 12% (1.3 BBOE) |
| Cretaceous/ Jurassic | | 165 | | 1% | 3% (0.5 BBOE) | — |

Figure 3.  Lower Tertiary trend stratigraphic section in the deepwater Gulf of Mexico.

Figure 4 illustrates the extent of the Lower Tertiary trend.  The trend stretches from west to east over 450 mi and may reach up to 100 mi from north to south.  The trend may cover over 30,000 mi$^2$ (77,700 km$^2$) at an average depth of 25,000 ft (7,620 m) subsea, much of it hidden below a thick canopy of salt. With only 12 announced discoveries and one extended well test to date, defining and delineating this trend will be an active exploration and appraisal activity for several years to come.

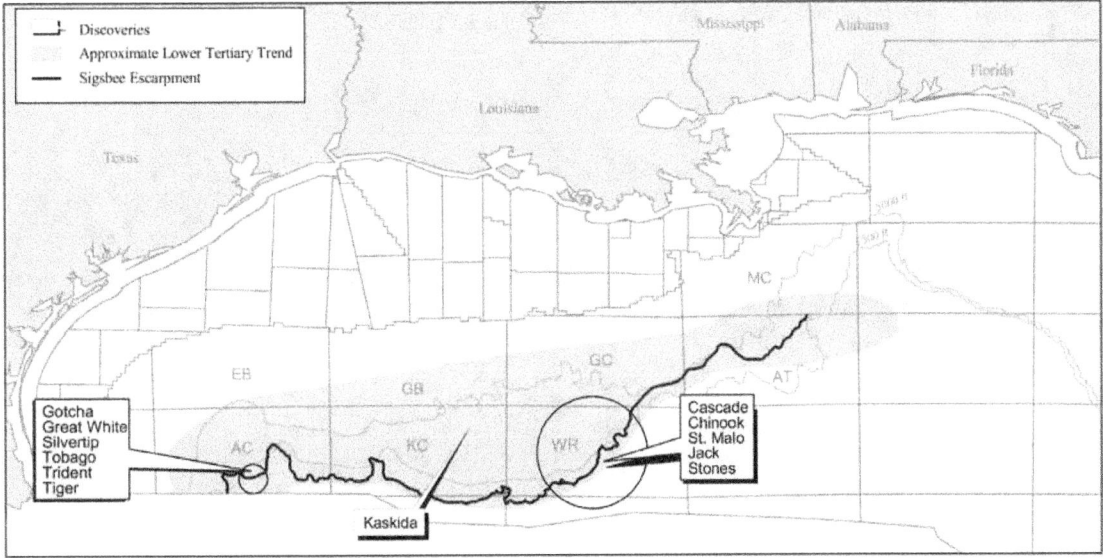

Figure 4.  Lower Tertiary trend in the deepwater Gulf of Mexico.

Figure 5 is a depth-migrated seismic line across the Lower Tertiary trend. The first section identified in light blue in the graphic is the overlying salt. The salt has a very high velocity when compared with the surrounding rocks, and a correction for this high velocity zone must be made to best image the sediments below the salt. This correction is essential to generate an accurate depth map, locate wells, and delineate the limits of a potential oil and gas field. The objective lower Tertiary section is depicted in light gray and, at least on this single line, many trapping opportunities may be identified. This seismic line demonstrates the complex shape of the overlying salt and the difficulty of correcting for its high velocity. This line also demonstrates the challenges in drilling and testing many of the lower Tertiary prospects (also true for similar upper Tertiary subsalt wells). These challenges include

- very deep waters,
- a thick overlying salt layer,
- target depths below 25,000 ft (7,620 m), and
- the potential for high pressure and high temperature conditions.

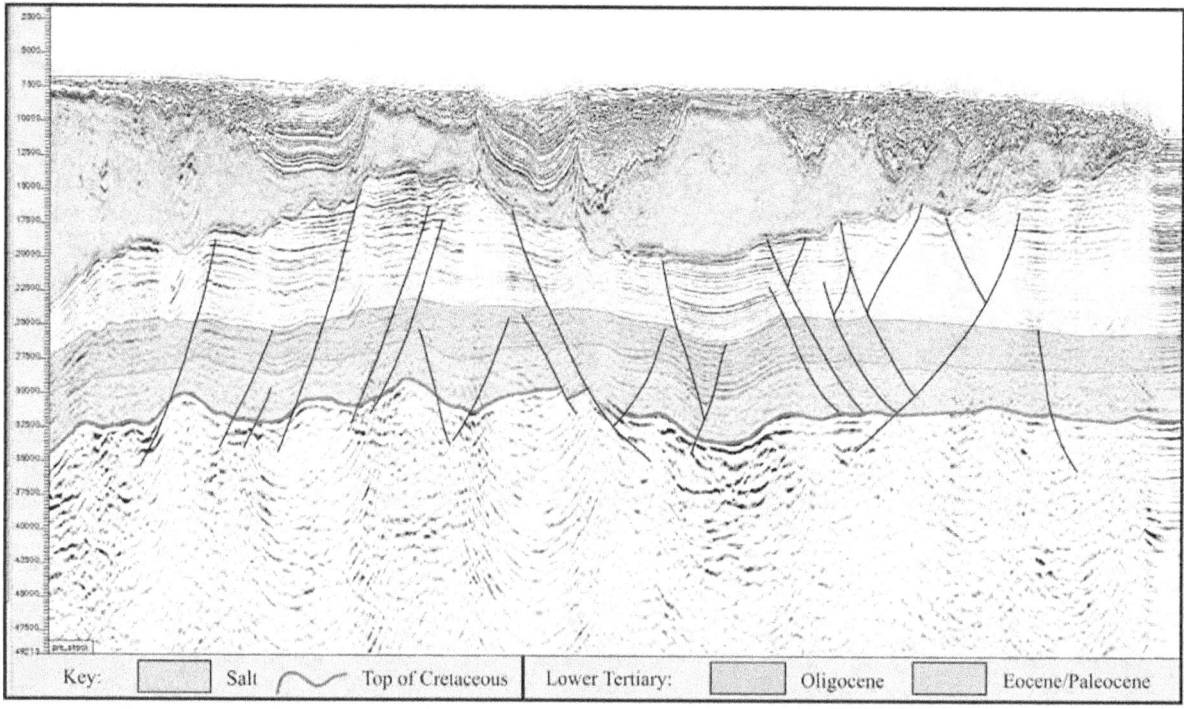

Figure 5. Lower Tertiary trend seismic line. (Data shown by permission from CGGVeritas.)

The Lower Tertiary trend lies mostly in water depths of 4,000 to over 7,500 ft (1,219 to over 2,286 m) (figure 4). Drilling depths greater than 32,000 ft (9,754 m), high temperature, high pressures, and thousands of feet of overlying salt can drive well costs to $80-120 million. The availability of rigs capable of drilling these wells is limited, and with rig-on-location times of 3-6 months to drill each well, further delays in drilling additional prospects are created. This delay results in greater demands for rigs and is likely to lead to even higher well costs.

In 2006, British Petroleum (BP) announced that a well drilled at their Kaskida prospect encountered a significant amount of hydrocarbon-bearing section. Located in the north-central part of Keathley Canyon Block 292, the Kaskida prospect bridged the gap between the earlier Alaminos Canyon discoveries to the west and the more recent Walker Ridge discoveries to the east, as well as extended the play northward. Below are excerpts from BP's news release of August 31, 2006, regarding their Kaskida prospect.

> BP America Inc. announced an oil discovery on an exploration well which tested the Kaskida prospect in the Gulf of Mexico. The well, located on Keathley Canyon block 292, is in about 5,860 feet of water and is about 250 miles southwest of New Orleans. Kaskida was drilled to a total depth of approximately 32,500 feet in the lower tertiary and encountered 800 net feet of hydrocarbon-bearing sands.
>
> "Appraisal will be required to determine the size and commerciality of the discovery," said David Rainey, Vice President Gulf of Mexico Exploration. "We expect to return to Kaskida later this year to commence appraisal activity." (BP, 2006)

Last year, too, Chevron used the Transocean Inc.'s *Cajun Express* drilling rig to perform an extended well production test on the Jack 2 well in Walker Ridge Block 758 (figure 6). Results from this test were eagerly awaited by companies involved in the Lower Tertiary trend. The discovery at the Jack prospect was announced in September 2004 and the results of the extended well test at Jack 2 were announced by Chevron in September 2006. This extended well test set depth and pressure records and took three months to complete at an estimated cost of $100 million (Mufson, 2006). An excerpt from Chevron's September 5, 2006, news release follows.

> Chevron Corporation announced today that it successfully completed a record setting production test on the Jack #2 well at Walker Ridge Block 758 in the U.S. Gulf of Mexico. The Jack well was completed and tested in 7,000 feet of water, and more than 20,000 feet under the sea floor, breaking Chevron's 2004 Tahiti well test record as the deepest successful well test in the Gulf of Mexico. The Jack #2 well was drilled to a total depth of 28,175 feet.
>
> The test was conducted during the second quarter of 2006 and was designed to evaluate a portion of the total pay interval. During the test, the well sustained a flow rate of more that 6,000 barrels of crude oil per day with the test representing approximately 40 percent of the total net pay measured in the Jack #2 well. Chevron and its co-owners plan to drill an additional appraisal well in 2007. (Chevron, 2006)

The Jack 2 test results are being analyzed to determine if these Lower Tertiary trend reservoirs are capable of sustained production at economic rates.

Figure 6. The *Cajun Express* rig used for the Jack 2 well production test. (Photo courtesy of Chevron.)

The results of the Jack 2 test re-intensified industry's interest surrounding the Lower Tertiary trend. The extended production test at the Jack 2 well provides encouragement that this trend will be able to produce very large hydrocarbon volumes. There are several contributing factors to support optimism about the Lower Tertiary trend's true hydrocarbon potential. The estimates of billions of barrels of producible oil and gas are justified, given the ratio of discoveries to dry holes, the thickness of the hydrocarbon-bearing columns encountered, the size and number of untested structures, and the recent Jack 2 well test results.

Industry has responded to the encouraging news from the Jack and the Kaskida discoveries not only by leasing new blocks but also by paying some of the highest bonuses ever seen in the adjacent areas. The Keathley Canyon area had five of the largest bids in Sale 200, with BP's Keathley Canyon Block 58 bid of $21 million the largest bonus offered. In fact, 38 percent of the tracts bid on in Sale 200 had Lower Tertiary potential, and these high bids represent approximately 63 percent of all dollars bid in the sale (USDOI, MMS, 2006a). Industry's very active acquisition of new, high bonus leases is indicative of the potential many companies see in the trend.

The infrastructure needed to develop and deliver the deepwater production from these remote areas to market remains in the planning stages and will require a consortium of companies to dedicate hundreds of millions of dollars in capital expenditures. Shell and its partners have plans for the "Perdido Regional Development" located in Alaminos Canyon Block 857 for the Great White, Silver Tip, and Tobago discoveries. Highlights from the Shell press release for the Great White development follow.

> Shell Offshore Inc. (Shell) announced today that it will develop the Great White, Tobago and Silvertip Fields via a Perdido Regional Development host, located in Alaminos Canyon, offshore Gulf of Mexico, approximately 200 miles south of Freeport, TX. Moored in about 8,000 feet of water, the regional DVA (direct vertical access) spar will be the deepest spar production facility in the world. First production from Perdido is expected around the turn of the decade, with the facility capable of handling 130,000 boe/d.

8

The concept for regional development includes a common processing hub in Alaminos Canyon Block 857 near the Great White discovery that incorporates drilling capability and functionality to gather, process and export production within a 30-mile radius of the facility. This concept will provide regional synergies, reduced cost and lower risk. This regional concept will also reduce the number and size of the facilities and operations in this challenging frontier area, resulting in a lower environmental impact than would otherwise be achieved.

"The Perdido Foldbelt is remote and is located in ultradeep waters from about 7,500-10,000 feet, with rugged seafloor terrain," explained Marvin Odum, Executive Vice President, EP Americas. "This geologic setting is different from what has previously been produced in the Gulf of Mexico and will establish the first production from the Lower Tertiary (Paleogene) play in the Gulf of Mexico." (Shell, 2006)

Petrobras is planning to use an FPSO vessel to develop the Cascade and Chinook fields in Walker Ridge. Petrobras' FPSO may be ready for deployment in late 2009. The press release for the Cascade and Chinook developments reads in part as follows.

The plan consists of the installation and operation of a FPSO vessel in approximately 8,200 feet of water. The plan provides for at least two subsea wells in Cascade and one subsea well in Chinook, each drilled to an approximate depth of 27,000 feet and to be tied back to the FPSO. Based on reservoir performance, the development plan could be expanded to include additional wells on each unit. (Petrobras, 2006)

In summary, the presence of pre-Miocene reservoirs and discoveries in the ultra-deepwater demonstrates the continuing exploration and development potential in the deepwater GOM. These new plays are large in areal extent, have multiple opportunities, and contain potentially huge traps with the possibility of billions of barrels of hydrocarbons.

## CHALLENGES AND REWARDS

Deepwater operations are very expensive and often require significant amounts of time from the initial exploration activities to first production from the fields. Despite these challenges, deepwater operators often reap great rewards. Figure 7 shows the history of discoveries in the deepwater GOM. There has been a shift toward deeper water over time, and despite the challenges of deepwater drilling, the number of deepwater discoveries continues to increase, with 12 discoveries added in 2006, as seen in table 1 (in the Introduction).

In addition to the significant number of deepwater discoveries, the flow rates of deepwater wells and the field sizes of deepwater discoveries are often quite large (figure 8). These factors are critical to the economic success of deepwater development. In addition to their large sizes, deepwater fields have a wide geographic distribution and range in geologic age from Pleistocene through Paleocene.

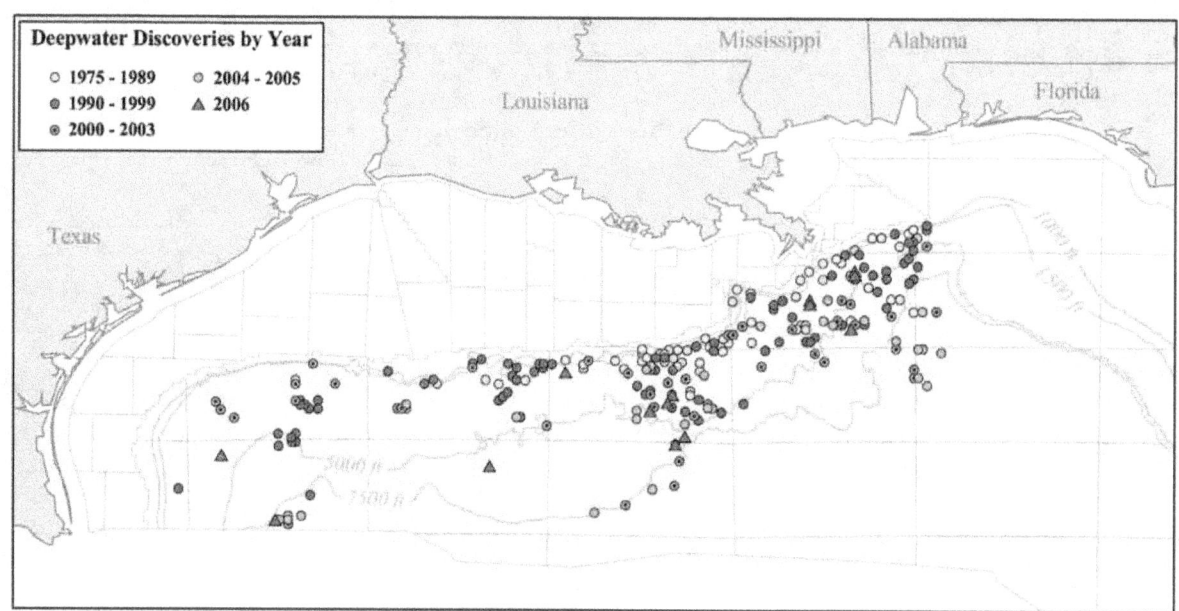

Figure 7.   Deepwater discoveries by year.

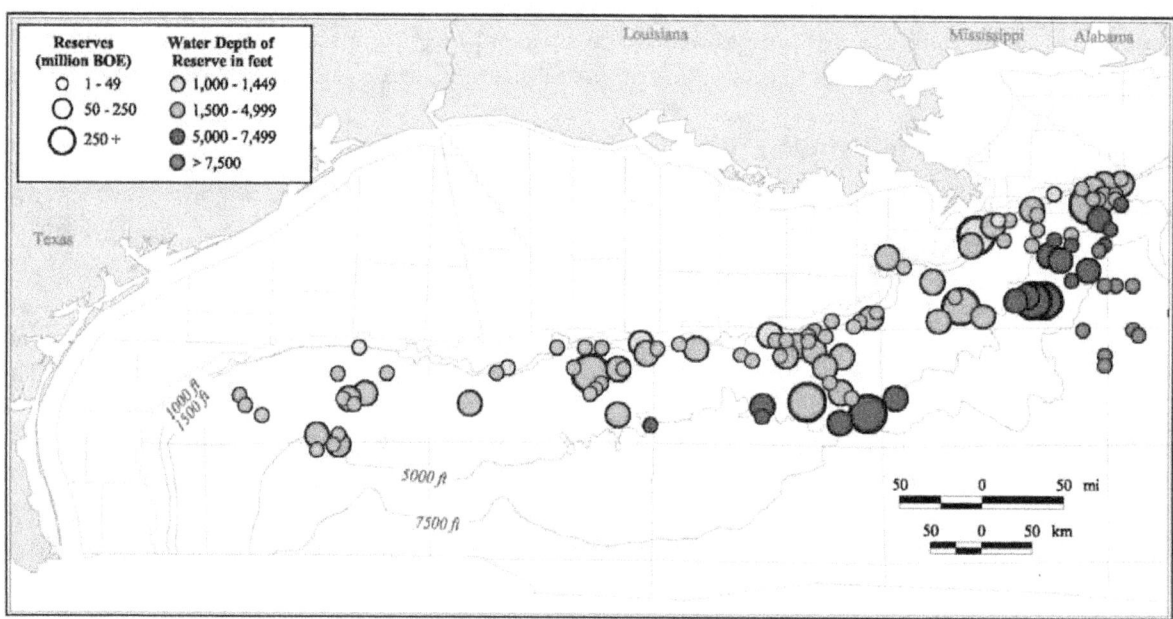

Figure 8.   Estimated volume of proved deepwater fields.

Table 2 depicts the deepwater discoveries in the Gulf in water depths greater than 7,500 ft (2,286 m). Note that many of these discoveries are associated with Independence Hub.

Table 2
List of Deepwater Discoveries in Water Depths Greater than 7,500 ft (2,286 m)

| Project Name | Area/Block | Water Depth (ft) | Discovery Year |
|---|---|---|---|
| Camden Hills | MC 348 | 7,530 | 1999 |
| Merganser* | AT 37 | 8,064 | 2001 |
| Trident | AC 903 | 9,816 | 2001 |
| Cascade | WR 206 | 8,143 | 2002 |
| Vortex* | AT 261 | 8,422 | 2002 |
| Atlas* | LL 50 | 9,180 | 2003 |
| Chinook | WR 469 | 9,104 | 2003 |
| Jubilee* | AT 349 | 8,891 | 2003 |
| Spiderman/Amazon* | DC 621 | 8,100 | 2003 |
| Atlas NW* | LL 5 | 8,810 | 2004 |
| Cheyenne* | LL 399 | 8,987 | 2004 |
| Mondo Northwest* | LL 2 | 8,340 | 2004 |
| San Jacinto* | DC 618 | 7,850 | 2004 |
| Silvertip | AC 815 | 9,226 | 2004 |
| Tiger | AC 818 | 9,004 | 2004 |
| Tobago | AC 859 | 9,627 | 2004 |
| Mondo NW Extension* | LL 1 | 8,340 | 2005 |
| Jubilee Extension* | LL 309 | 8,774 | 2005 |
| Stones | WR 508 | 9,556 | 2005 |
| Q* | MC 961 | 7,925 | 2005 |
| Gotcha | AC 856 | 7,600 | 2006 |

AC = Alaminos Canyon    AT = Atwater Valley    DC = DeSoto Canyon
LL = Lloyd Ridge    MC = Mississippi Canyon    WR = Walker Ridge
*Projects associated with Independence Hub

# LEASING AND ENVIRONMENT

## INTRODUCTION

The Gulf of Mexico OCS is divided into the three sectors—the Western, Central, and Eastern Planning Areas (figure 9). Note that this figure displays the new planning area boundaries recently designated in the *Federal Register* (2006; 71 FR 1) by MMS.

Many of the data presented in this report are subdivided according to water depth. These divisions (1,000, 1,500, 5,000, and 7,500 ft) are also illustrated in figure 9, along with the new deepwater royalty relief zones (400, 800, 1,600, and 2,000 m) of the Energy Policy Act of 2005 for reference. Not all leases within a colored area are eligible for royalty relief because of the differing vintage of leases included within the area. As a whole, the new relief zones have not been incorporated into the statistical analyses in this report. Royalty relief volumes were changed with the passage of the Act.

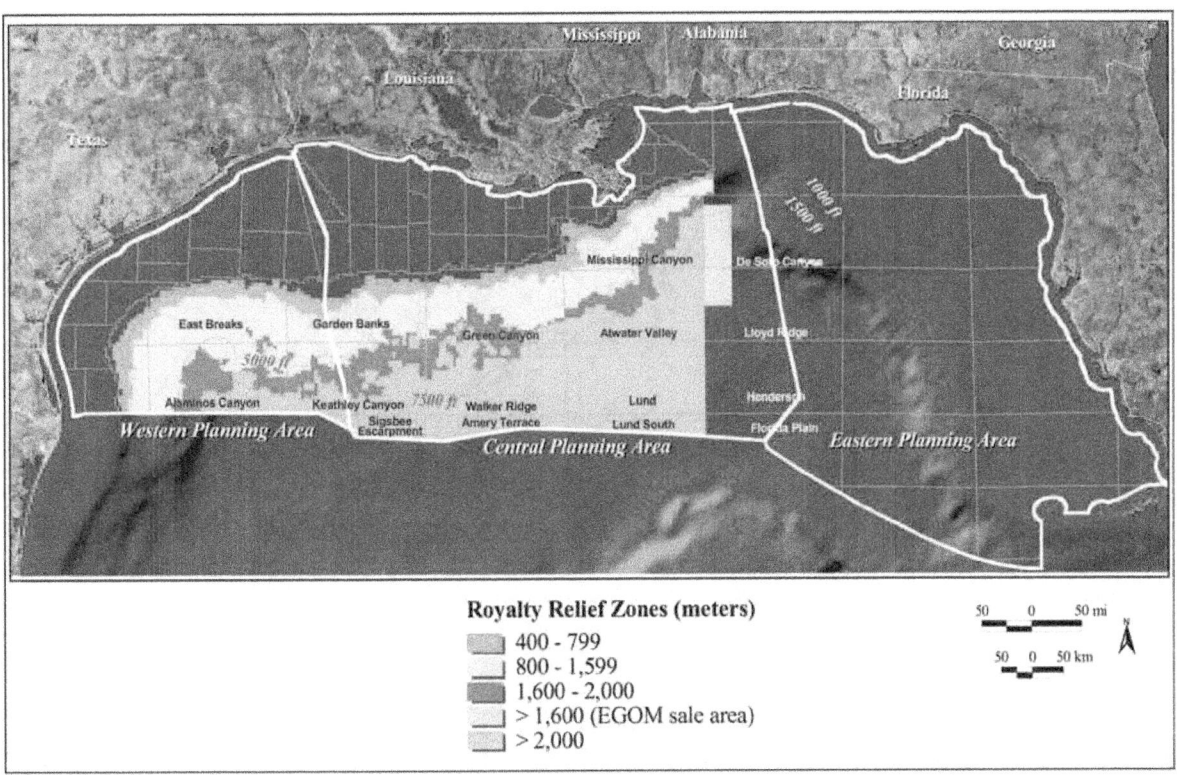

**Royalty Relief Zones (meters)**
- 400 - 799
- 800 - 1,599
- 1,600 - 2,000
- > 1,600 (EGOM sale area)
- > 2,000

Figure 9. Gulf of Mexico deepwater royalty relief zones.

## LEASING ACTIVITY

Figure 10 depicts all active leases in the GOM at the end of calendar year 2006. Note the great extent of leased blocks within the deepwater region. The pie chart inset in this figure highlights the relative percentage of active leases in each water-depth category. The limited number of active leases in the Eastern GOM is related to leasing restrictions. The approximate number of active leases for certain water-depth ranges is shown in table 3.

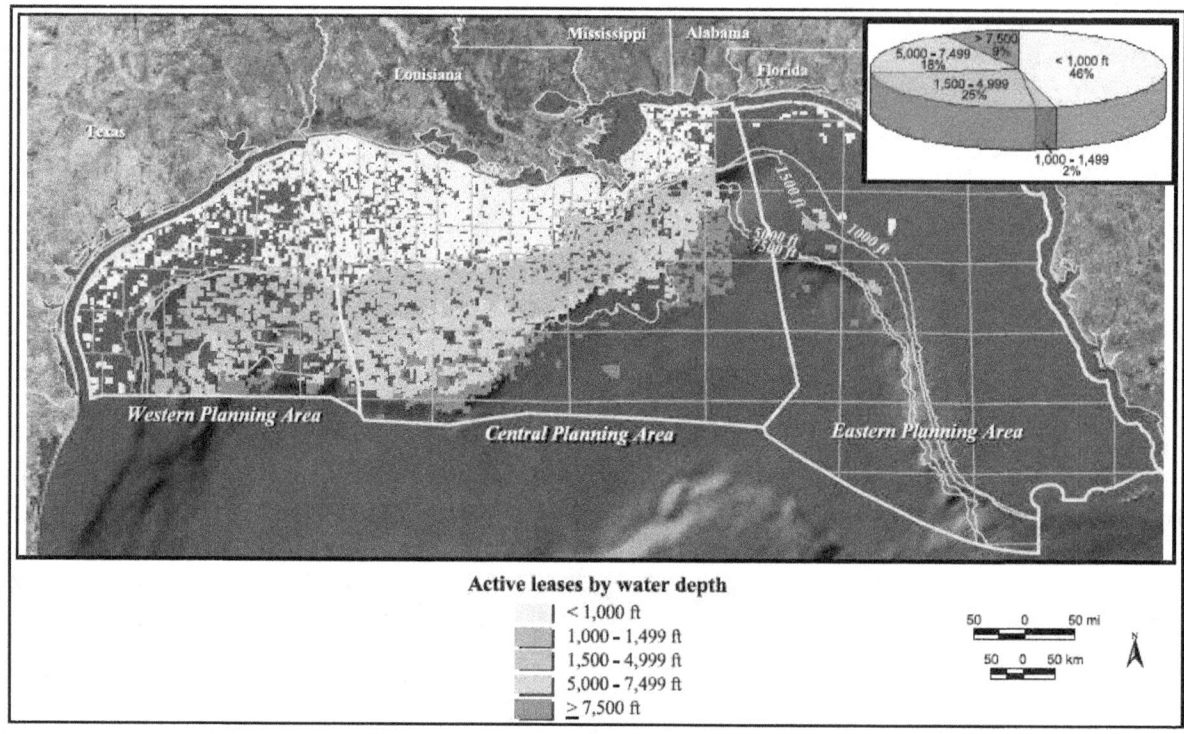

Active leases by water depth

| | < 1,000 ft |
| | 1,000 - 1,499 ft |
| | 1,500 - 4,999 ft |
| | 5,000 - 7,499 ft |
| | ≥ 7,500 ft |

Figure 10. Active leases by water depth.

Table 3
Number of Active Leases by Water-Depth Interval

| Number of | Water Depth | |
| Active Leases | ft | m |
| --- | --- | --- |
| 3,606 | <1,000 | <305 |
| 172 | 1,000-1,499 | 305-457 |
| 1,984 | 1,500-4,999 | 457-1,524 |
| 1,435 | 5,000-7,499 | 1,524-2,286 |
| 658 | >7,500 | >2,286 |

Data compiled as of 12/31/2006.

After enactment of the Deep Water Royalty Relief Act (DWRRA), deepwater leasing activity exploded in the Gulf. Other factors contributing to the increased activity included several key deepwater discoveries (including those recent discoveries in the Lower Tertiary trend), the recognition of high deepwater production rates, the evolution of deepwater development technologies, and a rise in oil and gas prices.

## LEASING TRENDS

The water-depth categories depicted in figure 11 reflect the divisions used in the DWRRA. In 2006, two lease sales were held—Sale 198 (Central GOM) and Sale 200 (Western GOM). Figure 11 includes the 763 leases issued from these sales.

14

Two water-depth ranges in figure 11 are worthy of discussion. The first is the less-than-200-m (656-ft) interval (the shelf). From 2000 through 2001, industry interest was rekindled in the traditional shelf blocks. From 2002, leasing activity at this water depth increased slightly through 2004. In 2005 and 2006, the number of leases issued on the shelf declined.

The second trend of note involves the greater-than-800-m (2,625-ft) interval. In 2006, the number of leases issued in water depths of greater-than-800 m eclipsed those in the less-than-200-m interval. From 2000 to 2003, a steady increase in the number of leases issued occurred in the greater-than-800-m water-depth interval (the peak in 2001 was the result of the addition of 95 Eastern GOM leases to those from the annual Central GOM and Western GOM sales). From 2004 to 2005, there was a leveling off of interest in the deeper waters. However, in 2006, the greater-than-800-m (2,625-ft) water-depth interval experienced a 17 percent increase from its 2005 level. That same year, the number of leases issued in the greater-than-800-m interval outpaced the number of leases issued in the less-than-200-m range by more than 30 percent.

Figure 12 was derived from the data in figure 11, but displays the deepwater categories used elsewhere in this report. (Shallow-water data are excluded from figure 12.) These deepwater data show the rapid increase in leasing activity that began in 1995 and continued through 1998. Although leasing activity plummeted in 1999, higher levels of leasing activity returned after 2000. Several factors initiated this resurgence, including high oil and gas prices and several major discoveries, such as Mad Dog and Thunder Horse. Two intervals are worthy of note—the 1,500-4,999 ft and 5,000-7,499 ft ranges. These intervals generally parallel each other with the 1,500-4,999 ft outpacing the deeper water range. From 1999 through 2003, the ranges steadily increased, then leveled off in 2004 and 2005, and began to climb again in 2006. From 2005 to 2006, the 1,500-4,999 ft interval increased 32 percent while the 5,000-7,499 ft range increased by 29 percent. These increases were likely caused by industry showing particular interest in Garden Banks and Keathley Canyon—more than 50 percent of the tracts that received bids in Sale 200 were located in these two areas. In this sale, about 38 percent of these tracts are believed to have a Lower Tertiary target, and the high bids on these tracts totaled 63 percent of all dollars bid in the sale (USDOI, MMS, 2006a).

## FUTURE LEASE ACTIVITY

Since the deepwater arena in the GOM is already heavily leased, the number of leases that will be relinquished, terminated, or expire will influence activity in future lease sales. Given the fact that most companies can drill only a small percentage of their active leases, it is likely that many high-quality leases will expire without being tested. The impending turnover of these leases often results in "farm-outs" to non-majors, opportunities for different companies to gain a lease position and, potentially, a more rapid exploration and development of the acreage. Ultimately, an untested and undeveloped lease will expire and possibly be leased again. Appendix E contains information about future sale dates.

Sale 200 (Western GOM) may be indicative of this trend. The high level of activity in this sale was sparked by the large number of newly available tracts offered for lease. There were 445 newly available tracts and, of them, 130 received bids in this sale. The Garden Banks and Keathley Canyon areas accounted for 61.5 percent (80 of the 130 newly available tracts) of those blocks that received bids.

15

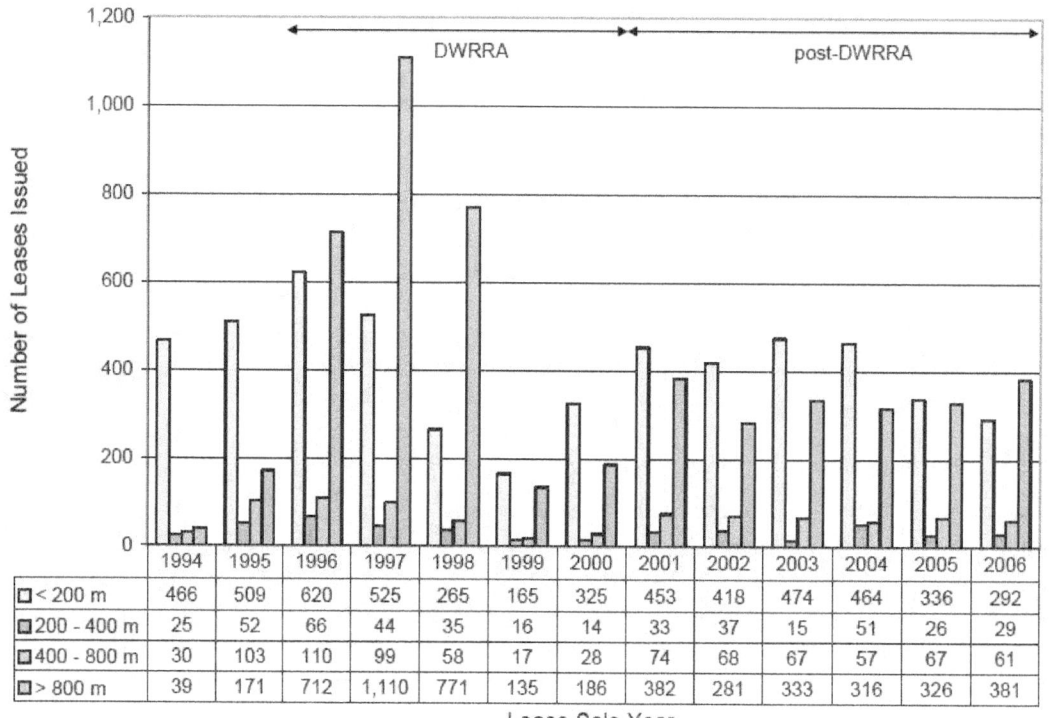

| Lease Sale Year | 1994 | 1995 | 1996 | 1997 | 1998 | 1999 | 2000 | 2001 | 2002 | 2003 | 2004 | 2005 | 2006 |
|---|---|---|---|---|---|---|---|---|---|---|---|---|---|
| □ < 200 m | 466 | 509 | 620 | 525 | 265 | 165 | 325 | 453 | 418 | 474 | 464 | 336 | 292 |
| ▨ 200 - 400 m | 25 | 52 | 66 | 44 | 35 | 16 | 14 | 33 | 37 | 15 | 51 | 26 | 29 |
| ▨ 400 - 800 m | 30 | 103 | 110 | 99 | 58 | 17 | 28 | 74 | 68 | 67 | 57 | 67 | 61 |
| □ > 800 m | 39 | 171 | 712 | 1,110 | 771 | 135 | 186 | 382 | 281 | 333 | 316 | 326 | 381 |

Figure 11. Number of leases issued each year, subdivided by DWRRA water-depth categories.

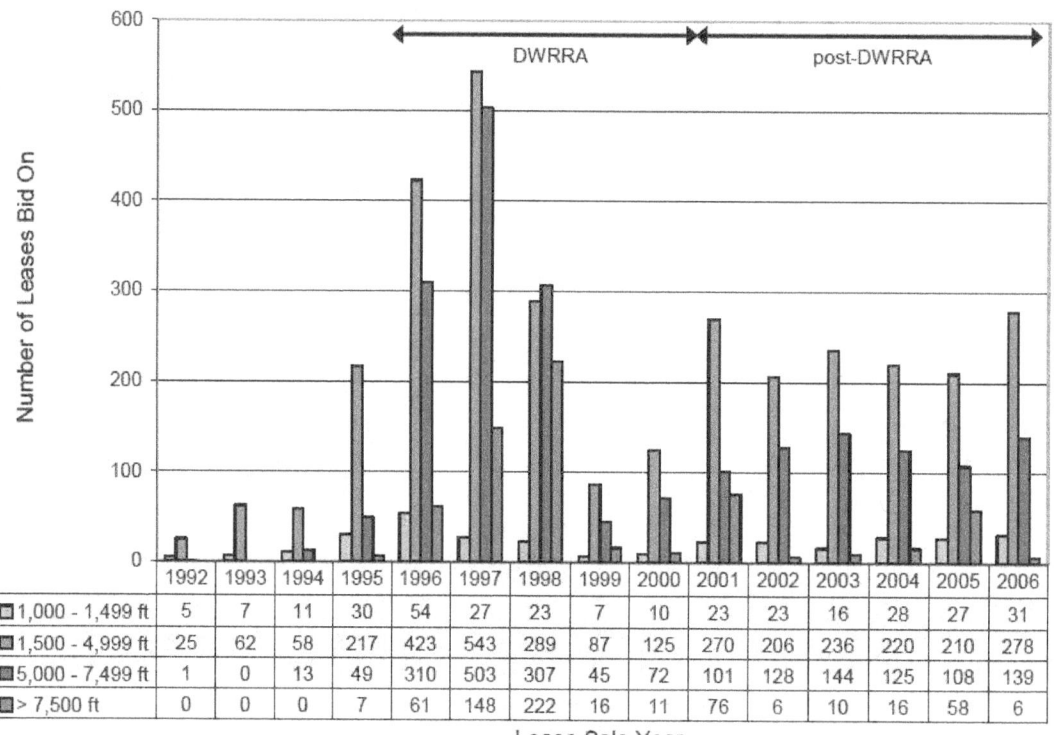

| Lease Sale Year | 1992 | 1993 | 1994 | 1995 | 1996 | 1997 | 1998 | 1999 | 2000 | 2001 | 2002 | 2003 | 2004 | 2005 | 2006 |
|---|---|---|---|---|---|---|---|---|---|---|---|---|---|---|---|
| □ 1,000 - 1,499 ft | 5 | 7 | 11 | 30 | 54 | 27 | 23 | 7 | 10 | 23 | 23 | 16 | 28 | 27 | 31 |
| ▨ 1,500 - 4,999 ft | 25 | 62 | 58 | 217 | 423 | 543 | 289 | 87 | 125 | 270 | 206 | 236 | 220 | 210 | 278 |
| ▨ 5,000 - 7,499 ft | 1 | 0 | 13 | 49 | 310 | 503 | 307 | 45 | 72 | 101 | 128 | 144 | 125 | 108 | 139 |
| ▨ > 7,500 ft | 0 | 0 | 0 | 7 | 61 | 148 | 222 | 16 | 11 | 76 | 6 | 10 | 16 | 58 | 6 |

Figure 12. Number of leases bid on for each deepwater interval.

Figures 13a and 13b show leases that will expire from 2006 to 2016 in two-year intervals. The data used in creating figures 13a and 13b assume that each lease expires at the end of its primary lease term (without a lease-term extension). Note that lease terms vary according to water depth. Primary lease terms are 5 years for blocks in less-than-400 m (1,312 ft), 8 years for blocks in 400-799 m (1,312-2,621 ft), and 10 years for blocks in 800 m (2,625 ft) or greater. The availability of previously leased blocks is expected to increase dramatically as a result of the leasing boom that began in 1996 and continued through 1998. For example, as a result of the large number of leases acquired in 1996 (see figure 11), there will be a proportionally large number of blocks available in the sales during 2007. An examination of the map for years 2007-2008 (figure 13a) provides a picture of the number and extent of the deepwater blocks that will be available for the first time in a decade.

Traditionally, the Central GOM lease sales have transpired in the spring of each year. However, the next sale, Sale 205, has been delayed and is tentatively scheduled for October 3, 2007. The MMS established a cutoff deadline of February 14, 2007, for inclusion of expired, relinquished, or terminated lease blocks for Sale 205. Central Planning Area (CPA) blocks that became available after that date were deferred until the next Central GOM lease offering (Sale 206).

The MMS has also begun its proposed OCS Oil and Gas Leasing Program: 2007-2012 (5-Year Program). The 5-Year Program is the basis for the MMS's overall leasing activities on the OCS. It identifies the areas to be offered for leasing during the 5-year period and it establishes the schedule for individual lease sales. The Program proposes 11 oil and gas lease sales in the GOM—5 sales in the Western Planning Area (WPA) and 6 in the CPA. More information on the 5-Year Program may be gleaned from the following MMS web site: http://www.mms.gov/5-year/WhatIs5YearProgram.htm.

## REGULATORY ISSUES

### Royalty Rate Increases

On January 9, 2007, the Secretary of the Department of the Interior, Dirk Kempthorne, announced an increase in the royalty rate for new offshore deepwater Federal oil and gas leases (Kemthorne, 2007). The royalty rate was increased to 16.7 percent (1/6th) from the present 12.5 percent (1/8th) on deepwater leases. The change in rate will take effect with the first 2007 GOM lease sale.

### Gulf of Mexico Energy Security Act of 2006

On December 20, 2006, President Bush signed into law the Gulf of Mexico Energy Security Act of 2006 (GOMESA). Appendix F contains excerpts from the Act. The GOMESA removed leasing restrictions on certain areas of the GOM, it extended leasing moratoria on other areas in the GOM (figure 14), and it increased the distribution of offshore oil and gas revenues to producing coastal States.

The GOMESA defines two areas of the GOM—the 181 Area and the 181 South Area. Approximately 2 million acres (ac) of the 181 Area are located within the CPA and this area was included in the recent draft and final Multisale EIS's. The CPA portion of the 181 Area may be available for lease in Sale 205, which is tentatively scheduled for October 3, 2007.

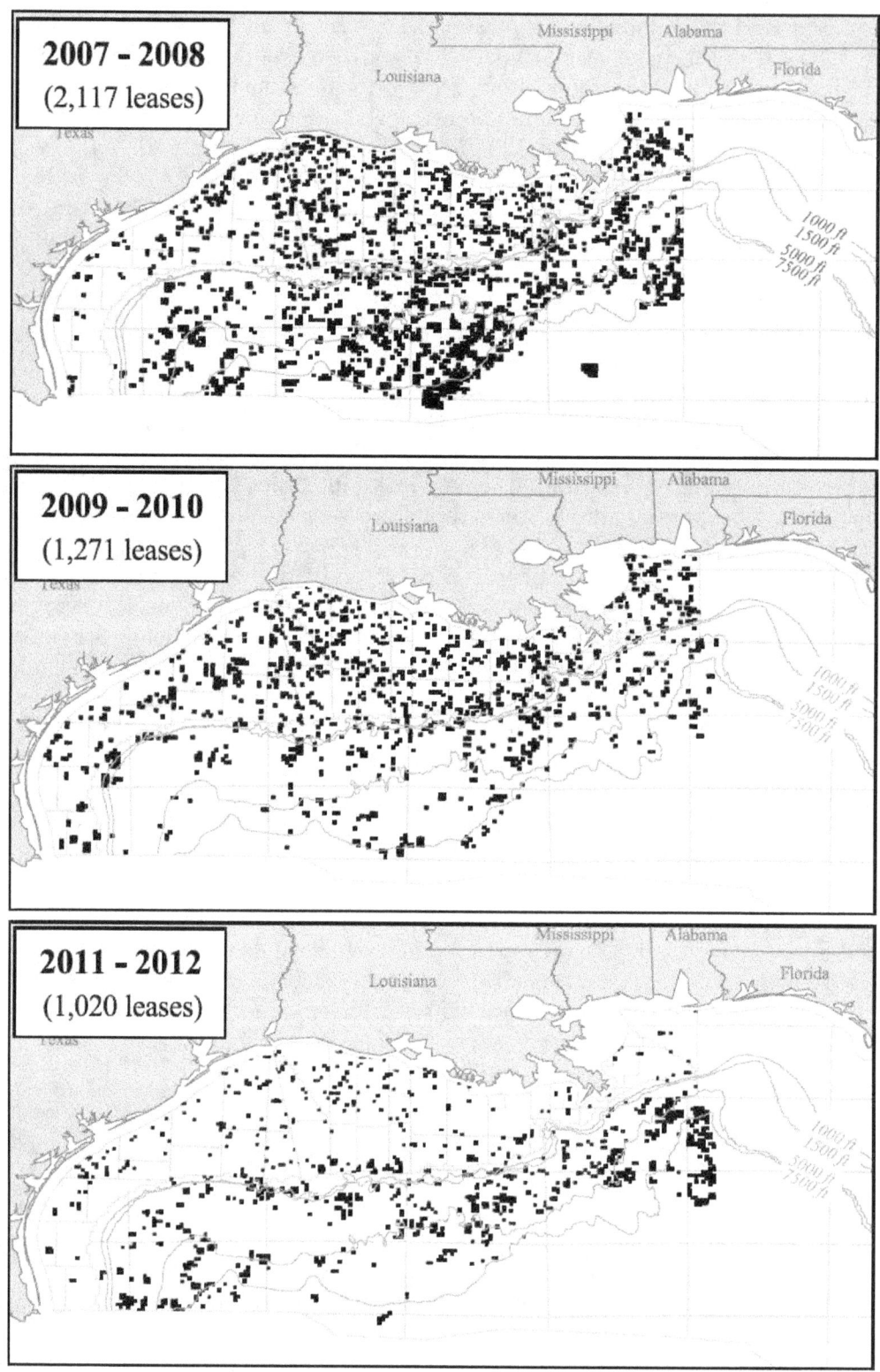

Figure 13a. Anticipated lease expirations from 2007 to 2012 in the Gulf of Mexico.

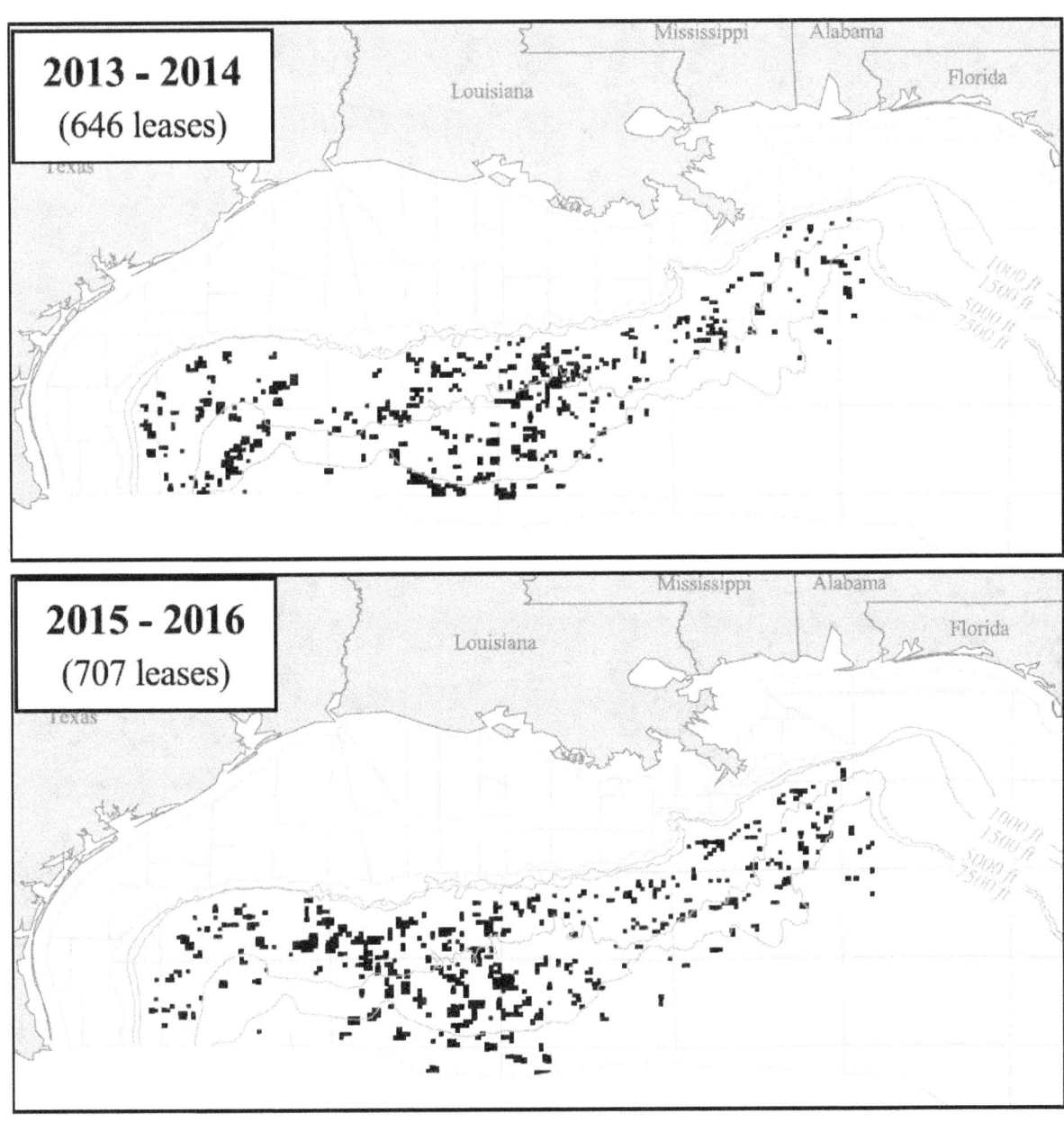

Figure 13b. Anticipated lease expirations from 2013 to 2016 in the Gulf of Mexico.

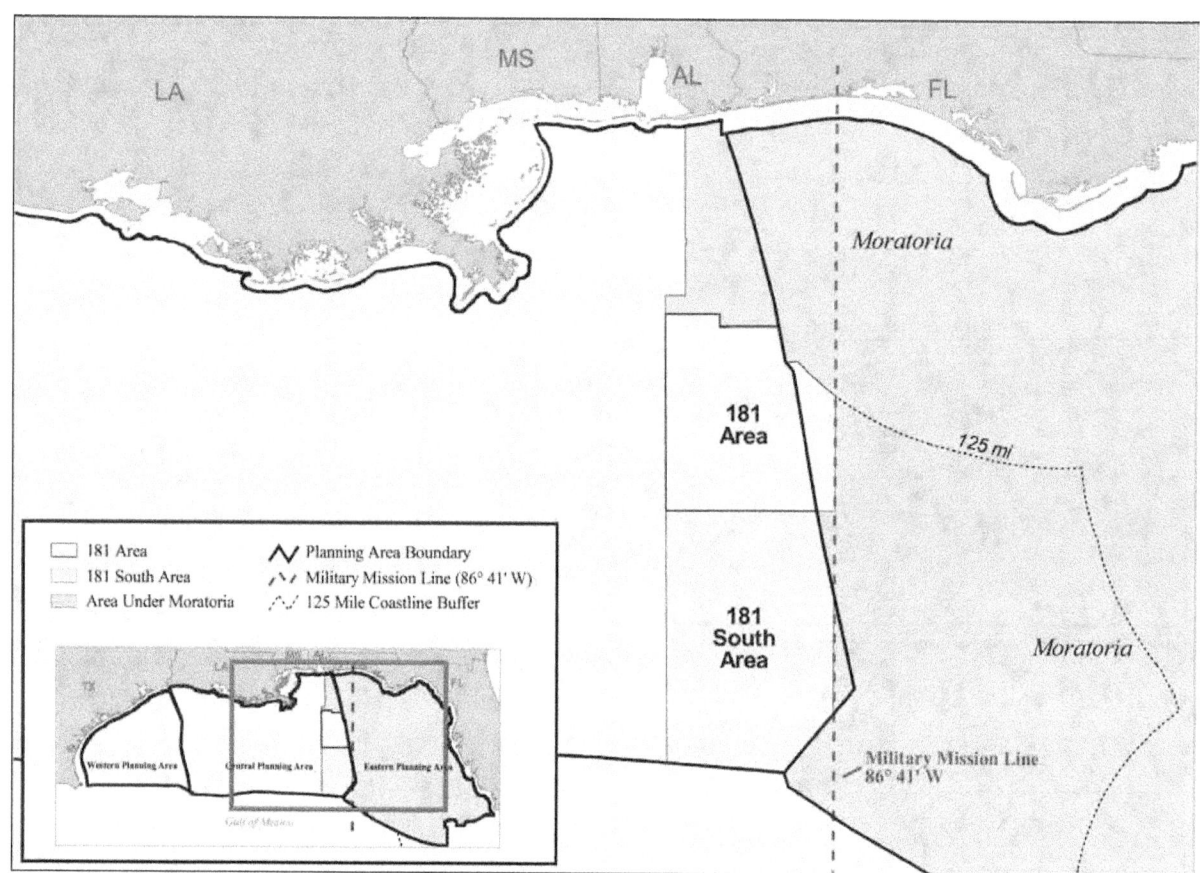

Figure 14. Map of the 181 Area and the 181 South Area.

The remaining portion of the GOMESA-defined 181 Area is located in the Eastern Planning Area (EPA) and it lies more than 125 mi from Florida. This area contains approximately 500,000 ac, is located west of the Military Mission Line (a north-south line at 86° 41' W longitude), and is tentatively scheduled to be offered in Lease Sale 224 in mid-March 2008. Sale 224 is planned to occur simultaneously with Sale 206, a CPA lease offering. The MMS announced in the *Federal Register* on February 14, 2007, its intent to prepare a supplemental EIS for Sale 224 (*Federal Register*, 2007; 72 FR 30).

The other area the GOMESA removed from leasing restriction is referred to as the 181 South Area. This area is located in the CPA and contains approximately 5.8 million acres. The MMS has not yet decided which proposed CPA lease sale would be the first to be expanded to include the 181 South Area. There are limited geological and geophysical data available to industry for this area and MMS believes that it would be premature to include the 181 South Area in either of the first two proposed CPA lease sales (Sale 205 in 2007 and Sale 206 in 2008). Prior to the GOMESA, the 181 South Area was under lease restrictions and was not included in the CPA proposed actions that were analyzed in the EIS. Once a decision is made to offer the 181 South Area, MMS will conduct a separate NEPA review to reevaluate the expanded CPA sale area.

President Bush modified the presidential withdrawal of the 181 South Area to be consistent with the GOMESA (Bush, 2007). (See appendix C.)

The GOMESA establishes a moratorium on leasing, pre-leasing, and other activities in the following areas until June 30, 2022:

- the area within 125 mi of the State of Florida in the EPA;

- the 181 Area in the CPA that is within 100 mi of the State of Florida; and

- the area east of the Military Mission Line (a north-south line at 86° 41′ W longitude).

The GOMESA also mandates that MMS provide an option to exchange existing leases located in the unavailable areas listed above for leases in the available areas of the GOM.

Prior to the GOMESA, affected States received recurring annual disbursements of 27 percent of royalty, rent, and bonus revenues received within each State's 8(g) zone. Beginning in FY 2007, and thereafter, Gulf producing States (i.e., Texas, Louisiana, Mississippi, and Alabama) will receive 37.5 percent of revenue from new leases issued in the 181 Area and 181 South Area. Beginning in FY 2016 and thereafter, Gulf producing States will receive 37.5 percent from new leases in the existing areas available for leasing. The remaining 50 percent and 12.5 percent of the total revenues would be distributed to the U.S. Treasury and the Land and Water Conservation Fund (LWCF), respectively.

## ENVIRONMENTAL ISSUES

### Ocean Current Monitoring

The most energetic currents in the Gulf of Mexico affect the ocean from its surface down to approximately the 3,281-ft (1,000-m) water-depth level with varying speeds. Currents as high as 4 knots (kn) have been observed from the surface to 1,000-ft (305-m) water depths. These upper currents taper off between 1,000- and 3,281-ft (305- and 1,000-m) depths.

Beneath the 3,281-ft (1,000-m) water-depth level, other currents migrate around the deep waters of the GOM. These deep currents were once thought to be minimal and were not a major consideration in most structure designs. In 1999, industry reported significant currents below 3,000 ft (914 m). This information led to a Safety Alert (USDOI, MMS, 2000; Notice No. 180) and subsequent studies of deep currents by MMS (Hamilton et al., 2003; Hamilton et al., 2000). These studies revealed significant deep currents of up to 2 kn at some locations.

The Hamilton et al. investigations spawned another deepwater current study funded by MMS—the "Exploratory Study of Deepwater Currents in the Gulf of Mexico" (Donohue et al., 2006a; Donohue et al., 2006b). Figure 15 shows the location of various instrument sites used during this study.

In the study, oceanographers investigated an area off the Mississippi Delta, where deepwater currents are known to concentrate. In this area, high-velocity currents develop in waves lasting for different periods. Those currents that developed in waves that peaked every 10 days are reflected into the deepwater Gulf rather than moving west along the coast as would typically be expected. However, there are less powerful currents that develop in waves peaking every 20 or 30 days. The initial findings indicate that these longer period waves move westward.

The study confirmed that there are two layers of currents. The top layer is more powerful. In motion near the bottom, however, there are "small" eddies some 50-70 km in size. The study also confirmed that there is a high energy current in front of and over the Sigsbee Escarpment, a steep section of the continental slope offshore Louisiana and Texas. The escarpment blocks that high energy current from moving onto the Continental Slope.

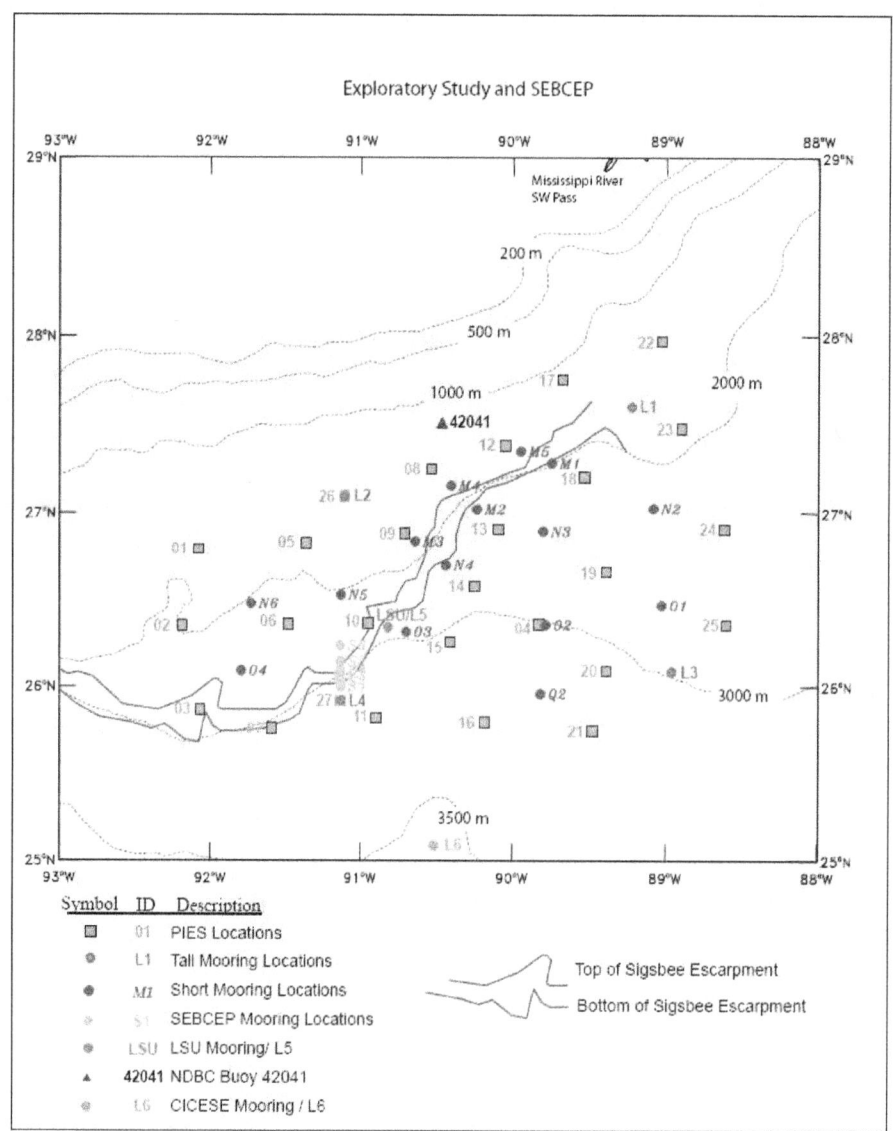

Figure 15. General bathymetric map showing the location of various instrument sites used during the Exploratory Study (Donohue et al., 2006b).

"This new study has added significant findings to the growing knowledge of physical oceanography," states Chris Oynes, Associate Director of Offshore Minerals Management. "It is very useful because engineers can use this information to design offshore platforms and facilities that can withstand these deepwater currents." The study also made use of bottom current measurements collected by the oil and gas industry as part of the study's database. Additional information is available at the Region's website, http://www.gomr.mms.gov.

Incidents have occurred in the deepwater areas of the Gulf that demonstrate the need for more accurate data in hindcasting and forecasting events and in daily operations. The MMS initially issued a Notice to Lessees and Operators (NTL) (2004-G21) in November 2004, which was superseded by NTL 2005-G02 (USDOI, MMS, 2005), "Deepwater Ocean Current Monitoring on Floating Facilities." The NTL implemented a program where operators of deepwater offshore production facilities and mobile offshore drilling units (MODU's) collect data on ocean currents and submit them for publication on an industry-sponsored Internet website. Data collected on currents may improve fatigue forecast models and help establish responsible design criteria, resulting in increased reliability of deepwater structures, thereby reducing risk to human lives, offshore facilities, and the ocean environment.

To understand better the physical oceanographic conditions in the GOM, MMS has participated in two industry groups since 1998—the Climate and Simulation of Eddies group (CASE) and the Eddy Joint Industry Project group (EJIP). The efforts of these two groups have been merged and their assets combined to form a single new group, CASE/EJIP. The group sponsors numerical modeling of the GOM deepwater circulation, which helps MMS understand important processes when observations are limited or unavailable. It also helps MMS to construct a robust climatology of deepwater processes. The group maintains a database that is very useful in supplementing other deepwater data available to MMS.

## Grid Programmatic Environmental Assessments

A biologically based grid system was developed by MMS as part of its comprehensive strategy to address deepwater issues. The grid system initially divided the Gulf into 17 areas or "grids" of biological similarity (figure 16). Another grid was added to the system to address the modified Sale 181 area, making a total of 18 grids for the Gulf. Under this strategy, MMS will prepare a Programmatic Environmental Assessment (PEA) that analyzes a proposed development project within each of the grids and that characterizes the whole grid. These grid PEA's are comprehensive in terms of the impact-producing factors and in terms of the environmental and socioeconomic resources described and analyzed for the entire grid. They also address potential cumulative effects of proposed projects within the grid. Other information on publicly announced projects within the grid is discussed, as well as any potential effects expected from future developmental activities. Projects selected for the PEA's are representative of the types of development expected for the grid. For example, a good candidate for a PEA would be a proposed development of a new surface structure that might serve as a "hub" for future development within the grid.

Once a grid PEA has been completed, it will serve as a reference document to implement the "tiering" and "incorporation by reference" concepts detailed in the implementing regulations of the National Environmental Policy Act (NEPA). Future environmental evaluations may reference appropriate sections from the PEA to reduce duplication of issues and effects addressed in the grid NEPA document. This will allow the subsequent environmental analyses to focus on specific issues and effects related to the proposals.

Table 4 shows the status of the grid PEA's.

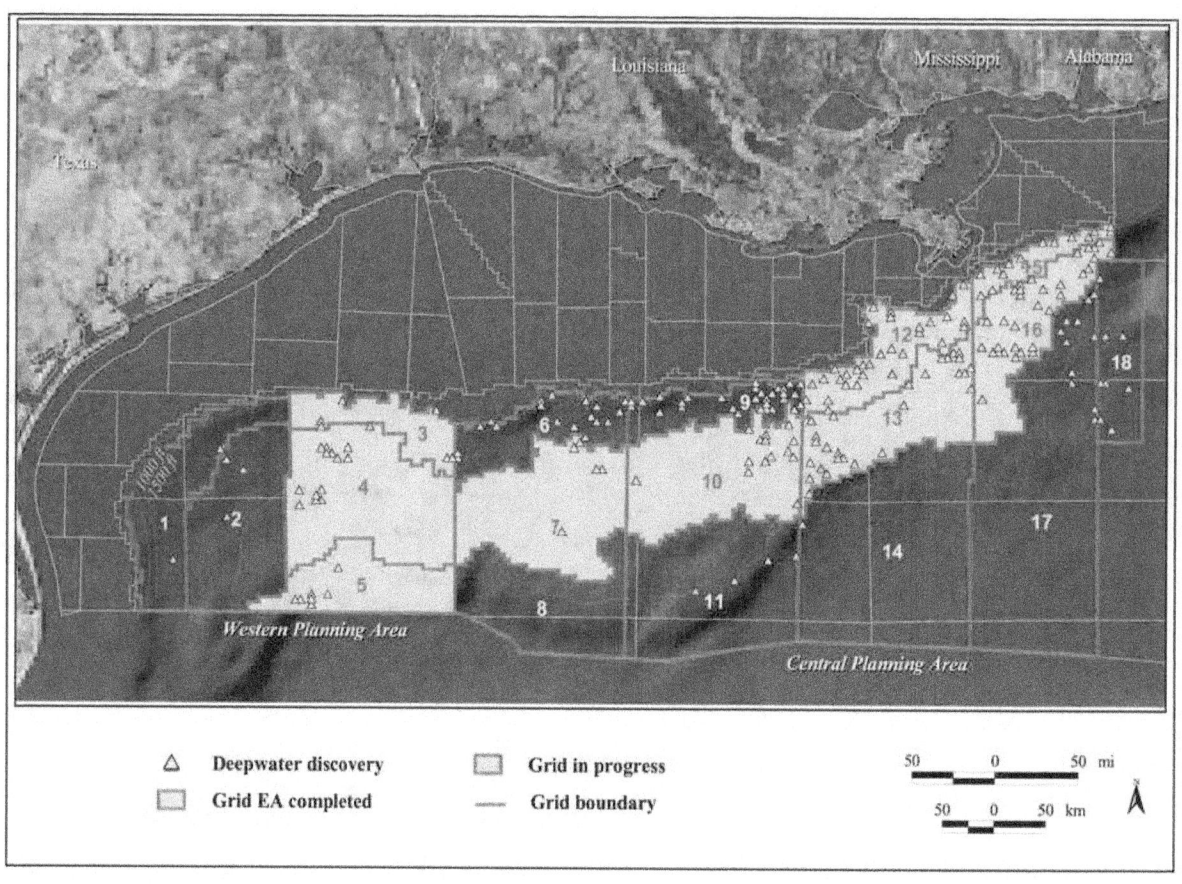

Figure 16. Grid PEA status.

Table 4
Grid PEA's Status Within the Central and Western Planning Areas of the Gulf of Mexico

| Grid | Project Name | Company | Plan | Area and Blocks |
|------|-------------|---------|------|-----------------|
| 3 | Gunnison | Kerr-McGee | N-7625 | GB 667, 668, & 669 |
| 4 | Nansen | Kerr-McGee | N-7045 | EB 602 & 646 |
| 5* | Perdido | Shell | N-8809 | AC 812, 813, 814, & 857 |
| 7 | Magnolia | Conoco | N-7506 | GB 783 & 784 |
| 10 | Holstein | BP | N-7216 | GC 644 & 645 |
| 12 | Medusa | Murphy | N-7269 | MC 538 & 582 |
| 13 | Marco Polo | Anadarko | N-7753 | GC 608 |
| 15 | Matterhorn | TotalFinaElf | N-7249 | MC 243 |
| 16 | Thunder Horse | BP | N-7469 | MC 775-778 & 819-822 |

* Grid 5 PEA is in progress     AC = Alaminos Canyon     EB = East Breaks
GB = Garden Banks     GC = Green Canyon     MC = Mississippi Canyon

# DRILLING AND DEVELOPMENT

The MMS continually evaluates its regulations to determine which ones need revisions. The latest sets of updates occurred in the 30 CFR 250 and 282 regulations: Oil and Gas and Sulfur Operations in the Outer Continental Shelf—Plans and Information (*Federal Register*, 2005; 70 FR 167). These changes are effective for all plans received after January 1, 2006. The MMS has also prepared two NTL's that further clarify the informational requirements for plans—NTL 2006-G14 (Information Requirements for Exploration Plans and Development Coordination Documents) (USDOI, MMS, 2006b) and NTL 2006-G15 (Guidelines for Submitting Exploration Plans and Development Operations Coordination Documents) (USDOI, MMS, 2006c). A list of selected NTL's with 2006 effective dates is included in appendix D.

Figure 17 shows the number of deepwater Exploration Plans (EP's), deepwater Development Operations Coordination Documents (DOCD's), and Deepwater Operations Plans (DWOP's) received each year since 1992. Note that DWOP's requirements were initiated in 1995. The number of EP's, DOCD's, and DWOP's includes only the initial plans, not revisions or supplements to plans. In addition, the number of DWOP's received includes only initial Conceptual Plans or combined Conceptual Plans/DWOP's as allowed by the revised 30 CFR 250 Subpart B regulations. The MMS requires DWOP's for developments in water depths greater than 1,000 ft (305 m) and Conservation Information Documents (CID) for developments in water depths greater than 1,312 ft (400 m). Some shallow-water activities are included in the data because all subsea developments, regardless of water depth, must file a DWOP. The discussion of subsea wells that occurs later in this report will address the significance of shallow-water subsea tiebacks—the effective use of deepwater technologies in marginal developments.

One indicator that MMS has found useful in projecting activity levels is the number of plans received. Although the order of plan submission and drilling activities can vary with projects, operators generally proceed as follows:

- file an EP,
- drill exploratory wells,
- file a Conceptual Plan,
- file a DOCD and CID,
- file a DWOP,
- install production facilities,
- drill development wells, then
- begin first production.

There was a marked increase in EP's, DOCD's, and Conceptual Plans or combined Conceptual Plans/DWOP's beginning in 1996. Submittals of EP's reached a peak of 92 in 1999 and then hovered near 70 per year except for counts of 51 in 2004 and 2006. The number of DOCD submittals reached a high of 28 in 2005. There was an increase in the number of initial Conceptual Plans or combined Conceptual Plans/DWOP's submitted from 2004 to 2006 (from 29 to 43).

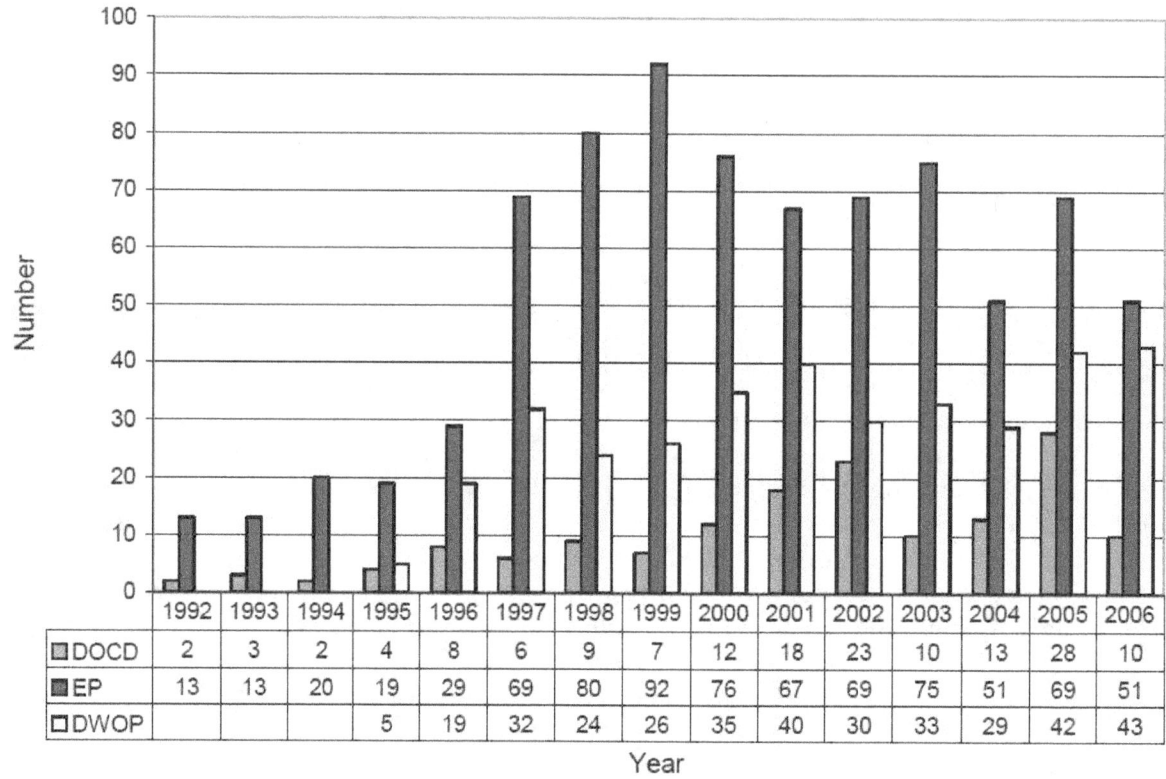

| | 1992 | 1993 | 1994 | 1995 | 1996 | 1997 | 1998 | 1999 | 2000 | 2001 | 2002 | 2003 | 2004 | 2005 | 2006 |
|---|---|---|---|---|---|---|---|---|---|---|---|---|---|---|---|
| ▣ DOCD | 2 | 3 | 2 | 4 | 8 | 6 | 9 | 7 | 12 | 18 | 23 | 10 | 13 | 28 | 10 |
| ■ EP | 13 | 13 | 20 | 19 | 29 | 69 | 80 | 92 | 76 | 67 | 69 | 75 | 51 | 69 | 51 |
| ▢ DWOP | | | | 5 | 19 | 32 | 24 | 26 | 35 | 40 | 30 | 33 | 29 | 42 | 43 |

Year

Figure 17. Deepwater EP's, DOCD's, and DWOP's received in the Gulf of Mexico since 1992.

The number of deepwater rigs operating in the GOM was 26 in 2004 and 2005, but rose slightly in 2006 to 30, as seen in figure 18. It should be noted that this figure includes rigs operating on deepwater production facilities and MODU's.

Numerous deepwater prospects will go undrilled as the primary lease terms expire caused, in part, by industry decisions to drill higher grade prospects, as well as the limited number of rigs available for deepwater drilling in the GOM. While many deepwater-capable drilling rigs are under long-term contractual agreements, efforts began in early 2005 to move rigs from other parts of the world to the GOM and to upgrade existing rigs. Four more rigs became available in 2006 as a result of these efforts.

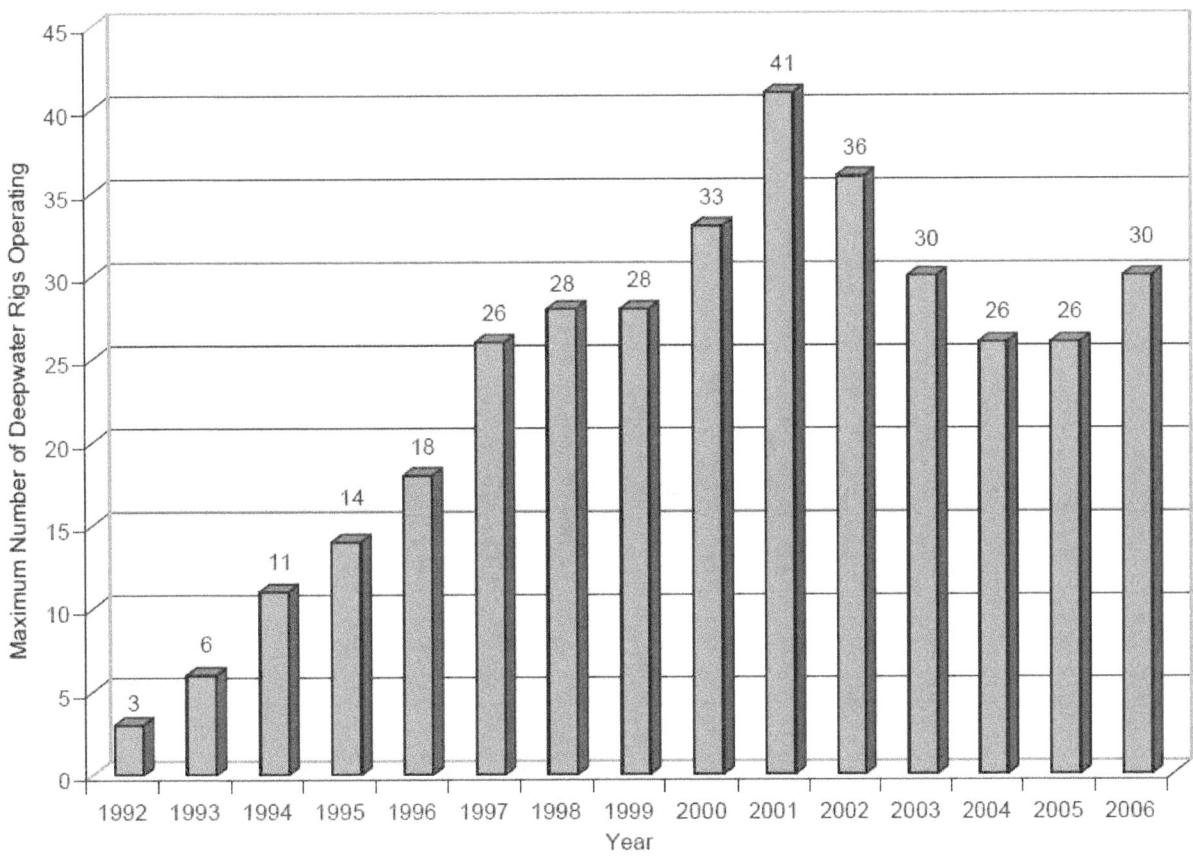

Figure 18. Maximum number of deepwater rigs operating in the Gulf of Mexico.

## DRILLING ACTIVITY

The number of deepwater wells drilled generally increased from 1992 through 2001, declined slightly to 2003, and has remained fairly flat since that time (figure 19).

Only original boreholes and sidetracks (a new bottomhole location) are included in the well counts used in this report. Wells defined as "by-passes" are specifically excluded. A "by-pass" is a section of well that does not seek a new objective; it is intended to drill around a section of the wellbore made unusable by stuck pipe or equipment left in the hole.

Figures 20 and 21 further delineate the deepwater well counts into exploratory and development wells, respectively. This report uses the designation of exploratory and development wells provided by the operators. The data reflect the variations among operators in classifying wells as either development or exploratory. After a decrease in 2002 and 2003, there was a significant increase in the number of exploratory wells drilled in 2004 through 2006. Exploratory drilling in all water depths increased in 2006. In the ultra-deepwater (> 7,500 ft or 2,286 m), 35 wells of all types were drilled in 2006, just missing the record set in 2004 by one well. There were nine exploratory wells drilled in the greater-than-7,500-ft (>2,286-m) water depth, a decrease of seven wells for that water depth since 2004. Although 2006 saw an increase in development wells over 2005, it was still below the peak reached in 2002.

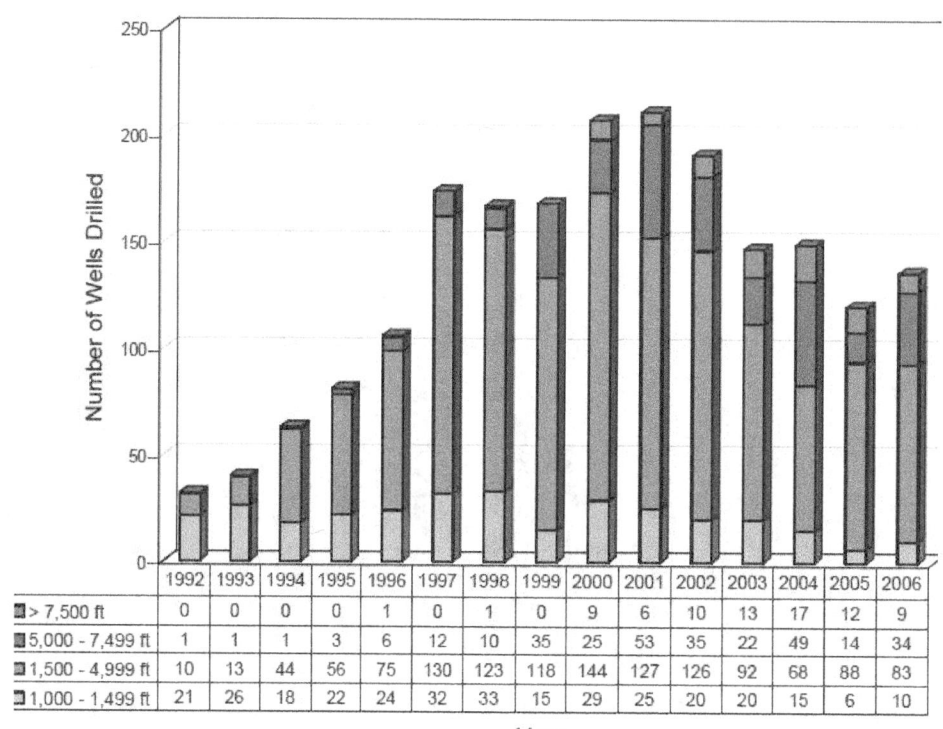

| | 1992 | 1993 | 1994 | 1995 | 1996 | 1997 | 1998 | 1999 | 2000 | 2001 | 2002 | 2003 | 2004 | 2005 | 2006 |
|---|---|---|---|---|---|---|---|---|---|---|---|---|---|---|---|
| ▪ > 7,500 ft | 0 | 0 | 0 | 0 | 1 | 0 | 1 | 0 | 9 | 6 | 10 | 13 | 17 | 12 | 9 |
| ▪ 5,000 - 7,499 ft | 1 | 1 | 1 | 3 | 6 | 12 | 10 | 35 | 25 | 53 | 35 | 22 | 49 | 14 | 34 |
| ▪ 1,500 - 4,999 ft | 10 | 13 | 44 | 56 | 75 | 130 | 123 | 118 | 144 | 127 | 126 | 92 | 68 | 88 | 83 |
| ▪ 1,000 - 1,499 ft | 21 | 26 | 18 | 22 | 24 | 32 | 33 | 15 | 29 | 25 | 20 | 20 | 15 | 6 | 10 |

Year

Figure 19.   All deepwater wells drilled in the Gulf of Mexico, subdivided by water depth.

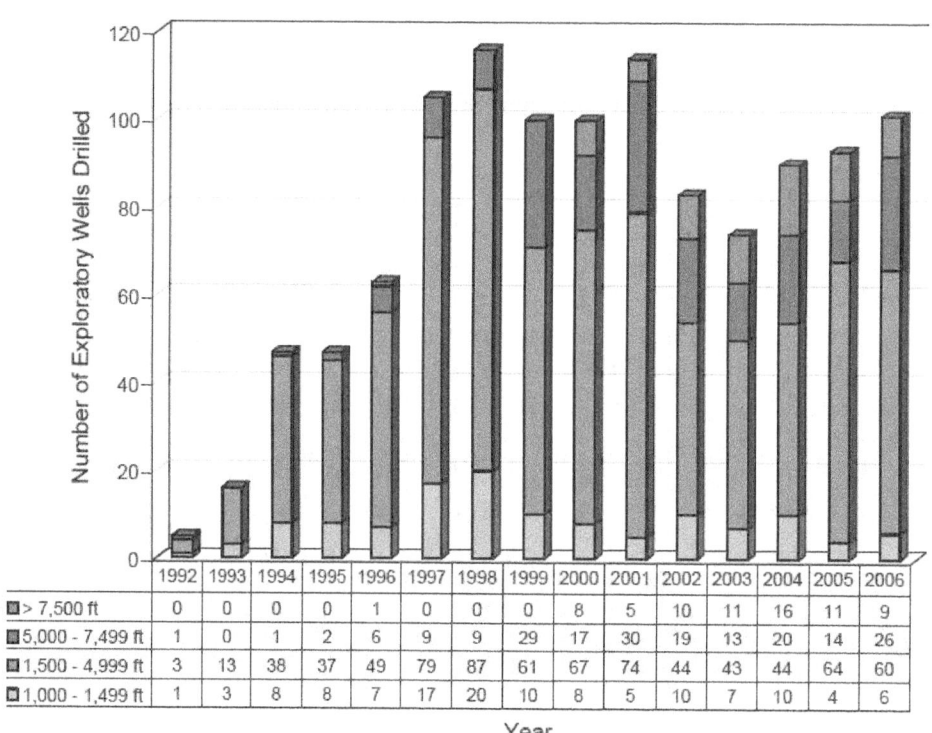

| | 1992 | 1993 | 1994 | 1995 | 1996 | 1997 | 1998 | 1999 | 2000 | 2001 | 2002 | 2003 | 2004 | 2005 | 2006 |
|---|---|---|---|---|---|---|---|---|---|---|---|---|---|---|---|
| ▪ > 7,500 ft | 0 | 0 | 0 | 0 | 1 | 0 | 0 | 0 | 8 | 5 | 10 | 11 | 16 | 11 | 9 |
| ▪ 5,000 - 7,499 ft | 1 | 0 | 1 | 2 | 6 | 9 | 9 | 29 | 17 | 30 | 19 | 13 | 20 | 14 | 26 |
| ▪ 1,500 - 4,999 ft | 3 | 13 | 38 | 37 | 49 | 79 | 87 | 61 | 67 | 74 | 44 | 43 | 44 | 64 | 60 |
| ▪ 1,000 - 1,499 ft | 1 | 3 | 8 | 8 | 7 | 17 | 20 | 10 | 8 | 5 | 10 | 7 | 10 | 4 | 6 |

Year

Figure 20.   Deepwater exploratory wells drilled in the Gulf of Mexico, subdivided by water depth.

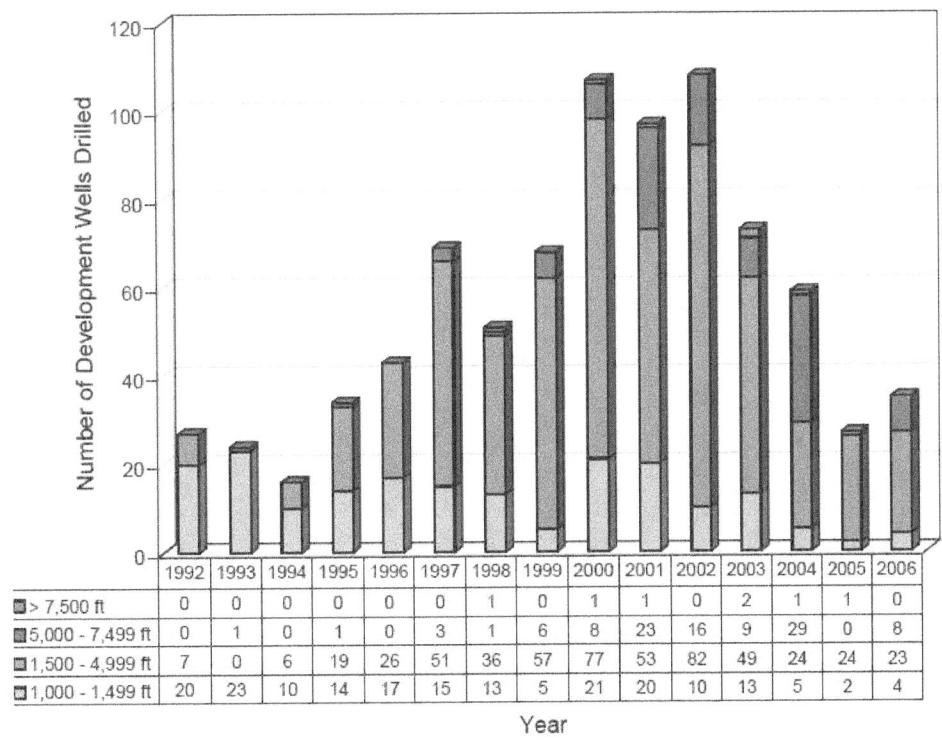

| | 1992 | 1993 | 1994 | 1995 | 1996 | 1997 | 1998 | 1999 | 2000 | 2001 | 2002 | 2003 | 2004 | 2005 | 2006 |
|---|---|---|---|---|---|---|---|---|---|---|---|---|---|---|---|
| ▣ > 7,500 ft | 0 | 0 | 0 | 0 | 0 | 0 | 1 | 0 | 1 | 1 | 0 | 2 | 1 | 1 | 0 |
| ▣ 5,000 - 7,499 ft | 0 | 1 | 0 | 1 | 0 | 3 | 1 | 6 | 8 | 23 | 16 | 9 | 29 | 0 | 8 |
| ▣ 1,500 - 4,999 ft | 7 | 0 | 6 | 19 | 26 | 51 | 36 | 57 | 77 | 53 | 82 | 49 | 24 | 24 | 23 |
| ▣ 1,000 - 1,499 ft | 20 | 23 | 10 | 14 | 17 | 15 | 13 | 5 | 21 | 20 | 10 | 13 | 5 | 2 | 4 |

Year

Figure 21. Deepwater development wells drilled in the Gulf of Mexico, subdivided by water depth.

# NEW TECHNOLOGY

The year 2006 was a banner year for the number of new technologies evaluated for use in offshore exploration and production operations. The MMS approved approximately 30 new technologies for use in the GOM. In addition, MMS and members of the industrial community have updated API recommended practices and other regulatory documents to accompany the technological advances.

Four examples of technology advancements that MMS approved in 2006 include a High Integrity Pressure Protection System (HIPPS); the use of pre-set polyester moorings for deepwater drilling rigs; various forms of subsea boosting, including a subsea pump that allows enhanced oil recovery; and a Conceptual Plan for a Floating Production, Storage, and Offloading (FPSO) facility.

## High Integrity Pressure Protection System (HIPPS) for Pipelines

Although a HIPPS system has not been proposed for a specific development, MMS did approve the general concept of a HIPPS system in July 2006, allowing the use of pipelines not rated for the well's full shut-in tubing pressure (SITP). The HIPPS employs valves, logic controllers, and pressure transmitters to protect the unrated section before the pipeline is over-pressured and/or ruptured, rather than relying on the physical strength of steel to withstand a well's SITP. The section of pipe upstream of the well and downstream of the HIPPS valves, as well as a short section of pipe upstream of the HIPPS valves, will be rated to the full SITP. This safety feature will provide an additional level of protection in case of a pressure spike and will allow time for the HIPPS logic system/valves to respond. Design and testing specifications have been defined for each section of the HIPPS system.

## Pre-set Polyester Moorings for MODU's

Although use of polyester mooring lines on production facilities is still considered new technology in the GOM, it is common practice to use this type of mooring line on MODU's. One stipulation for allowing the use of polyester moorings has traditionally been that the polyester rope may not come in contact with the seafloor in order to limit particle migration into the load-bearing fibers. In recent years, industry has requested that they be allowed to pre-set the mooring lines for MODU use since the lines can be inspected more frequently than for permanently fixed facilities. After conducting extensive research and studies on the jacket and filter layer of the polyester rope, MMS has granted approval for MODU's to pre-set polyester mooring lines with the stipulation that the lines be inspected and tested approximately every six months.

## Subsea Separation and Boosting System

A subsea separation and boosting system has also received conceptual approval to be used in the GOM. Shell Exploration and Production Company (Shell) has proposed a Separation and Boosting System (SBS) that will separate production fluids at the seafloor and direct them to the surface host via a pump at the base of a production riser for use at their Perdido Regional Development. BP Exploration & Production Inc. (BP) has also submitted and received approval to use electrically driven, subsea multi-phase pumps at their King field. The pumps will boost the operating system pressure, lowering flowing tubing pressures at each well, thereby increasing flow rates. This production increase will extend the field's life by approximately two years and increase ultimate recovery.

## Floating Production, Storage, and Offloading (FPSO) Facility

Another significant new technology application was approved in late 2006. A Conceptual Deepwater Operations Plan (Conceptual Plan) was approved for the use of an FPSO vessel. The Conceptual Plan, submitted by Petrobras America Inc., contained development information for Phase 1, which includes installation of an FPSO with two wells in the Cascade field and one well in the Chinook field. An FPSO is a ship-shaped vessel with a topside crude oil process plant and oil storage located in the hull. Oil will be offloaded from the vessel via a shuttle tanker, integrated tug barge (ITB), or articulated tug barge (ATB). A single point, disconnectable turret mooring system will be used to ensure the FPSO can sail away during hurricanes. The conceptual plan also incorporated other new technologies, including the use of free-standing hybrid risers (FSHR), and torpedo piles. Initial production from these fields is expected in 2009.

## Review Process

The four new technologies mentioned above are just a few that have been reviewed by MMS's petroleum and structural engineers. Approval was granted only after significant research and hazard analyses were conducted. The engineers considered many different conditions that can exist offshore and also confirmed that there was a proven effective method to shut-down operations in the case of a failure.

In 2006, MMS spent approximately $1.8 million funding research in offshore technology, which can range from developing improvements in design standards to studying the effectiveness of a testing methodology. Some of the results from these studies aided MMS engineers in approving new technologies. Other results have paved the way for updates and revisions to existing regulations and recommended practices.

Engineers at MMS participated in over 15 API committees and are actively involved in updates to the API's recommended practices (RP) and special projects. Examples of these efforts include API RP 2SK (Design and Analysis of Stationkeeping for Floating Structures), API RP 2I (In-Service Inspection of Mooring Hardware for Floating Structures), API RP 2T (Planning, Designing, and Constructing Tension Leg Platforms, Rev. 10 [Draft]), and the Hurricane Evacuation and Assessment Team (HEAT) document. The acceptance of new technologies and practices in 2006 was the result of Federal Government and industry cooperation supporting safe and efficient energy exploration and development.

## DEVELOPMENT SYSTEMS

Development strategies, including choice of platform type, must consider issues such as:

- reserve size and distribution,

- proximity to existing infrastructure,

- operating considerations such as well interventions (ability to re-enter a well for repairs and re-completions),

- prior company expertise with similar structures,

- economic considerations, and

- an operator's interest in establishing a production hub for the area.

Appendix A lists the systems that have begun production in the GOM. Fixed platforms (e.g., Bullwinkle) have economic water-depth limits of about 1,400 ft (427 m). Compliant towers (e.g., Petronius) may be considered for water depths of approximately 1,000-3,000 ft (305-914 m). Tension-leg platforms (e.g., Brutus and Marco Polo) are frequently used in 1,000- to 5,000-ft (305- to 1,524-m) water depths. Spars (e.g., Genesis), semisubmersible production units (e.g., Na Kika), and FPSO systems (e.g., Cascade/Chinook) may be used in water depths ranging up to and beyond 10,000 ft (3,048 m).

### Fixed Platform

A fixed platform consists of a welded tubular steel jacket, deck, and surface facility. The jacket and deck make up the foundation for the surface facilities. The jacket is secured by piles driven into the seafloor. The height of the platform is dictated by the water depth at the intended location. Once the jacket is secured and a deck installed, additional modules are added for drilling, production, and crew operations. Large, barge-mounted cranes are used in positioning and securing the jacket and for the installation of the topside modules. Economic considerations hinder development of fixed (rigid) platforms in water depths greater than 2,000 ft (610 m).

### Compliant Tower

A compliant tower consists of a narrow tower and a piled foundation. Unlike a fixed platform, a compliant tower has greater flexibility and can withstand large lateral forces by sustaining significant lateral deflections. It is usually deployed in water depths between 1,000 ft (305 m) and 2,000 ft (610 m).

## Tension-Leg Platform

A tension-leg platform (TLP) is a compliant structural system vertically moored and using buoyant components to maintain tension in the mooring system. ConocoPhillips successfully installed the deepest TLP in the world at Magnolia (Garden Banks Block 783) in December 2004 in 4,674 ft (1,425 m) of water.

## Semisubmersible Production Facility

A semisubmersible production facility is a floating system that may have drilling capabilities. It comprises the following major components: pontoons, columns, and a large deck. The pontoons and columns provide buoyancy to the system. Production equipment, living quarters, and storage space are assembled on the deck. Semisubmersibles are permanently moored, using various anchoring techniques, and can be operated in a wide range of water depths.

The world's largest semisubmersible production facility, the 59,500-ton Thunder Horse production, drilling, and quarters (PDQ) unit, arrived in the GOM in 2004 from Korea. The topside modules, fabricated in Morgan City, Louisiana, were installed in Ingleside, Texas. The sheer size of the Thunder Horse project has garnered worldwide interest. The distance from the base of the hull to top of the drill rig is just over 450 ft (137 m). The immense deck area is approximately 3 ac in area. The Thunder Horse unit was nearly four years in the making and will develop the largest discovery ever made in the GOM. When fully operational, the unit will be capable of producing an astounding 250 thousand barrels of oil per day (Mbopd) and 200 million cubic feet per day (MMcfpd). The installation of Thunder Horse (Mississippi Canyon Block 778) was delayed by Hurricane Dennis in 2005 and was installed in 2006.

The semisubmersible for the Atlantis project was moored in the fourth quarter of 2006 in Green Canyon Block 787 in a record water depth of 7,074 ft (2,156 m). Atlantis is the second largest semisubmersible in the world, smaller only than Thunder Horse. The Atlantis mooring system includes the longest continuous wire mooring ropes ever built. Twelve large steel canisters, called suction piles, are embedded in the ocean floor to anchor the facility in place. Part of the chain used in this mooring system is the largest of its type in the world.

## Spar

A spar is a vessel with a circular cross-section that sits vertically in the water and is supported by buoyancy chambers (hard tanks) at the top, a flooded midsection structure hanging from the hard tanks, and a stabilizing keel section at the bottom. A spar is held in place by a catenary mooring system, providing lateral stability. There have been three generations of spar designs in the GOM—classic spar, truss spar, and cell spar.

The first classic spar was installed in 1996 in 1,935 ft (590 m) of water in the Neptune field (Viosca Knoll Block 826). Other examples of a classic spar are Genesis and Hoover-Diana. The second generation of spar design is the truss spar. An example of a deepwater project using a truss spar design is Mad Dog (Green Canyon Block 782), which went on production in 2005. The third generation of spar design is the cell spar. In July 2004, Kerr-McGee began production from the world's first cell spar at Red Hawk (Garden Banks Block

877) in 5,334 ft (1,626 m) of water. Red Hawk is capable of producing 120 MMcfpd, with the flexibility to expand to 300 MMcfpd.

## Subsea Systems

Subsea systems are capable of producing hydrocarbons from reservoirs covering the entire range of water depths explored and developed by industry. Subsea systems continue to be a key component in the success in deepwater development. These systems are generally multi-component seafloor facilities that allow the production of hydrocarbons in water depths that would normally preclude installing conventional fixed or bottom-founded platforms. The subsea system can be divided into two major components: the seafloor equipment and the surface equipment. The seafloor equipment will include some or all of the following: one or more subsea wells, manifolds, control umbilicals, and flowlines. The surface component of the subsea system includes the control system and other production equipment located on a host platform that itself could be located many miles from the actual well locations.

Figure 22 shows the location of the various structure types in the deepwater GOM. Note that many of these structures support tiebacks from subsea completions.

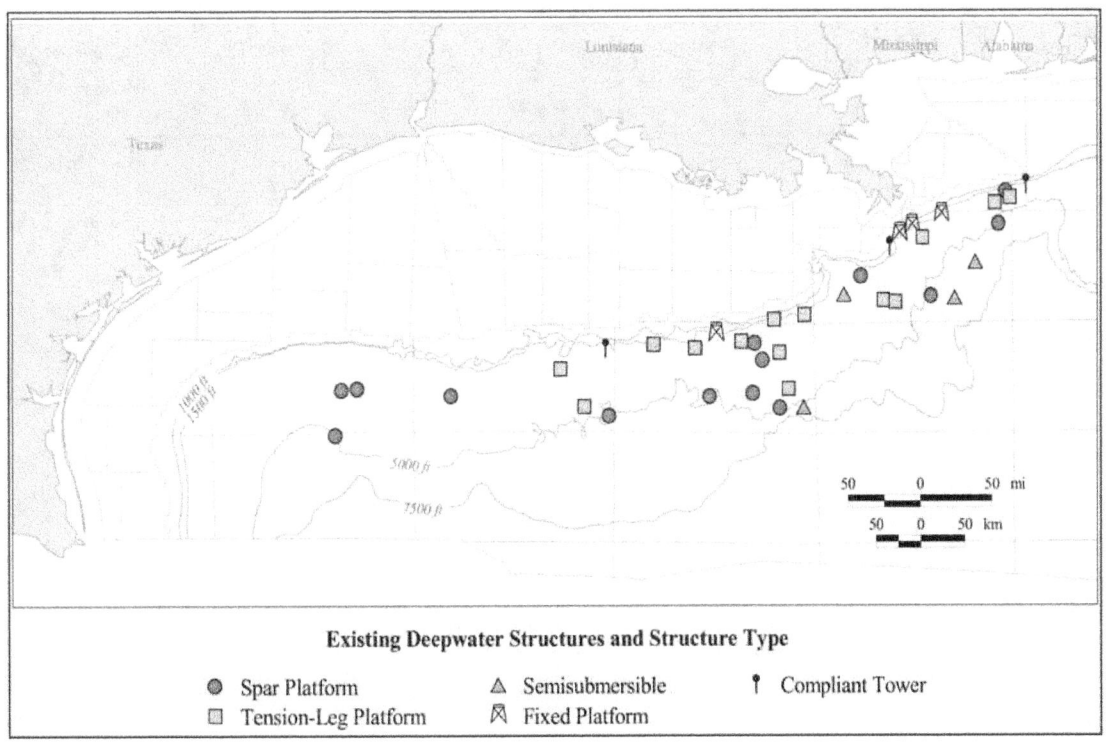

Figure 22. Location map of deepwater structures by type.

Some field discoveries in the deepwater GOM are too small to be economically developed as stand-alone projects. However, if they are located near an existing structure, they may use subsea completions that tieback their production to a hub facility. For purposes of this report, deepwater hubs are defined as surface structures that host production from one or more subsea projects. These hubs represent the first location where subsea production surfaces and are the connection point to the existing pipeline infrastructure. Note that

33

hubs are moving into deeper waters, expanding the infrastructure, and facilitating additional development in the ultra-deepwater frontier. Most hubs begin as stand-alone facilities (such as the Auger field) with later subsea tiebacks. Notable exceptions include Na Kika and Independence Hub, which were designed and located to support many smaller fields. Figure 23 shows the location of hub facilities in the deepwater GOM.

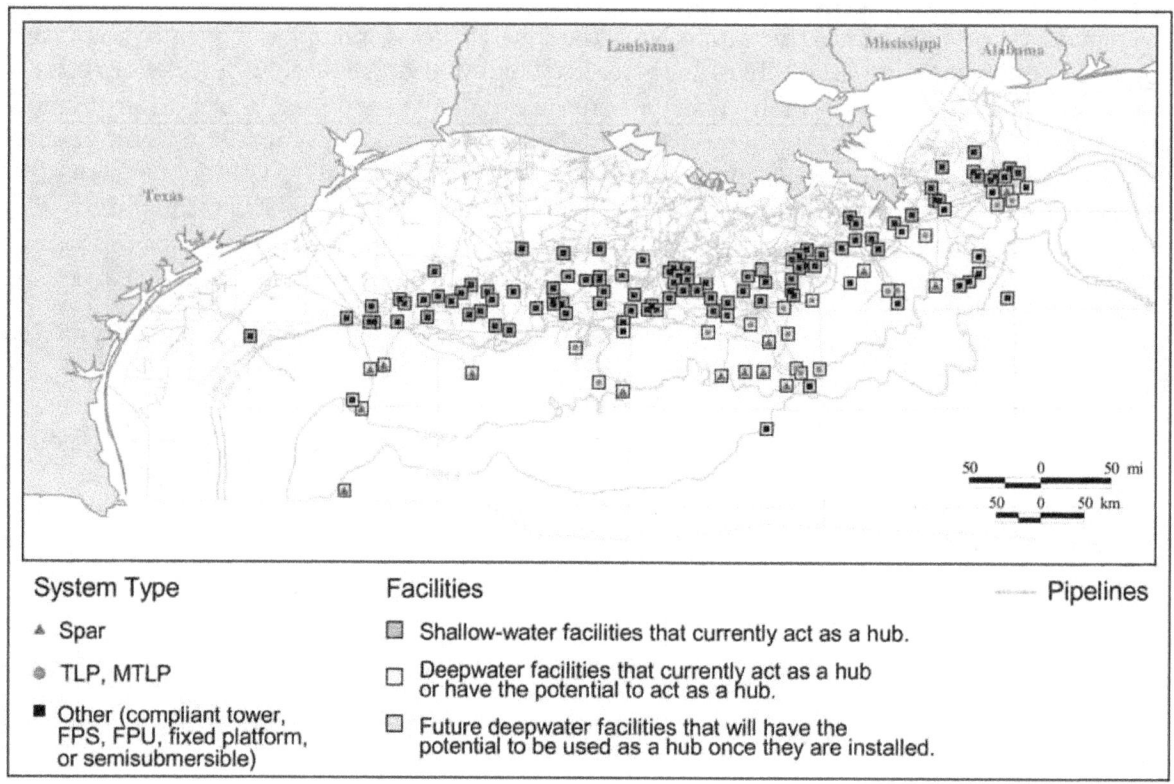

Figure 23. Current, potential, and future hub facilities in the Gulf of Mexico.

## INDEPENDENCE HUB

Independence Hub, LLC, an affiliate of Enterprise Products Partners L.P., has entered into agreements with the Atwater Valley Producers Group to gather natural gas from seven fields in the deepwater GOM. Atwater Valley Producers Group includes Anadarko Petroleum Corporation, Dominion Exploration & Production, Inc., Kerr-McGee Oil & Gas Corporation, Spinnaker Exploration Company, and Devon Energy Corporation. Enterprise Products Partners will design, construct, install, and own Independence Hub, and Anadarko will operate it.

Independence Hub is located on an unleased block, Mississippi Canyon Block 920, in a water depth of approximately 8,000 ft (2,438 m). The MMS granted a right of use and easement for this location. The selection of the location for the permanently moored host facility was based on seafloor conditions and proximity to these anchor fields: Atlas (Lloyd Ridge 50), Atlas NW (Lloyd Ridge 5), Jubilee (Atwater Valley 349), Merganser (Atwater Valley 37), San Jacinto (DeSoto Canyon 618), Spiderman (DeSoto Canyon 621), and Vortex (Atwater Valley 261). Murphy Oil's South Dachshund (Lloyd Ridge Block 2) discovery is also expected to be tied back to Independence Hub. The 105-ft (32-m) deep-draft, semisubmersible platform will have excess payload capacity that will allow the tieback of additional fields from other deepwater projects.  The facility will have capacity to produce approximately 1 billion cubic feet per day (Bcfpd).  The front cover of this report features a graphical representation of Independence Hub.

# RESERVES AND PRODUCTION

## DISCOVERIES

Figure 24 shows the number of deepwater discoveries each year since 1995. In an attempt to capture the impact of the deepwater exploratory successes, figure 24 includes industry-announced discoveries as well as MMS-known proved reserves, unproved reserves, and resource estimates. The industry-announced discovery volumes contain considerable uncertainty, are based on limited drilling, include numerous assumptions, and have not been confirmed by independent MMS analyses. They do, however, illustrate recent activity better than using only MMS-proved reserve numbers. The apparent decline of proved reserve additions in recent years is caused by the lag between discovery and development.[1]

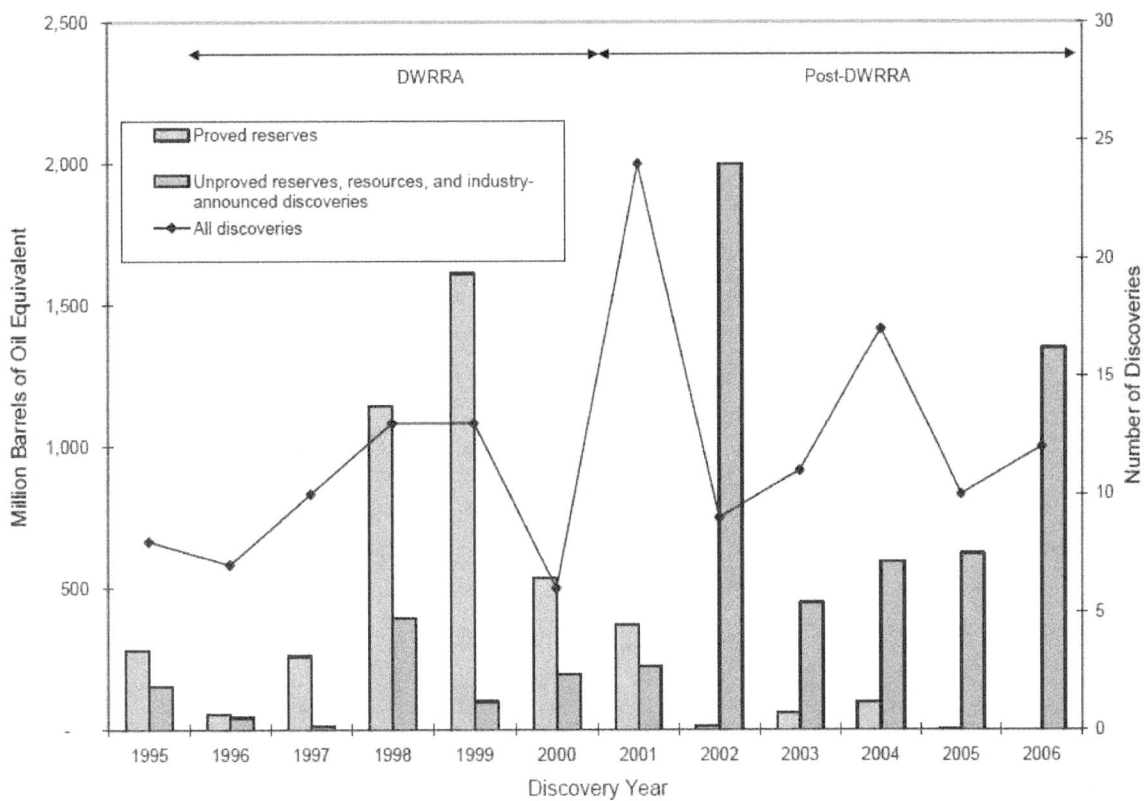

Figure 24. Number of deepwater discoveries (MMS reserves, MMS resources, and industry-announced discoveries).

## RESERVE POTENTIAL

A geologic-based estimate of future discoveries in the GOM is the 2000 Assessment (Lore et al., 2001). According to this document, the deepwater is expected to have ultimate reserves of approximately 71 BBOE, of which 56.2 BBOE remains to be discovered.[1] These

---

[1] The forecasts were based on the MMS report *Atlas of Gulf of Mexico Gas and Oil Sands* (Bascle et al., 2001).

estimates compare favorably with the shallow-water ultimate reserves of approximately 65 BBOE, of which 15.2 BBOE remains to be discovered. Note that the 2000 Assessment uses the DWRRA criteria (i.e., less than 200-m water depth is shallow water and greater than or equal to 200 m is deepwater).

## PRODUCTION TRENDS

Table 5 shows that 19 of the 20 most prolific producing blocks (on a BOE basis) are currently located in deep water.

Table 5
Top 20 Producing Blocks for the Years 2004-2005

| Block | Project Name | Operator | Water Depth (ft) | Production (BOE)* |
|---|---|---|---|---|
| MC 807 | Mars | Shell | 2,933 | 67,421,013 |
| MC 809 | Ursa | Shell | 3,800 | 47,560,888 |
| MC 127 | Horn Mountain | BP | 5,909 | 33,046,538 |
| GB 215 | Conger | Hess | 1,500 | 29,666,210 |
| MC 383 | Kepler (Na Kika) | BP | 5,759 | 29,302,884 |
| MC 765 | Princess | Shell | 3,600 | 26,821,862 |
| MC 763 | Mars | Shell | 3,261 | 26,378,385 |
| EB 602 | Nansen | Kerr-McGee | 3,675 | 24,834,539 |
| MC 522 | Fourier (Na Kika) | BP | 6,950 | 24,342,357 |
| VK 786 | Petronius | ChevronTexaco | 1,753 | 19,613,070 |
| GB 668 | Gunnison | Kerr-McGee | 3,100 | 18,100,007 |
| MC 429 | Ariel (Na Kika) | BP | 6,274 | 17,582,369 |
| EB 643 | North Boomvang | Kerr-McGee | 3,650 | 17,168,413 |
| GC 644 | Holstein | BP | 4,344 | 16,591,153 |
| EB 646 | Nansen | Kerr-McGee | 3,675 | 15,850,555 |
| MC 85 | King | BP | 5,689 | 14,603,185 |
| VK 915 | Marlin | BP | 3,236 | 13,897,605 |
| GC 243 | Aspen | Nexen | 3,065 | 13,722,419 |
| GB 341 | Habanero | Shell | 2,015 | 13,429,796 |
| ST 37 | Unnamed | ChevronTexaco | 59 | 12,971,079 |

*Cumulative production from January 2004 through December 2005.
EB = East Breaks          GB = Garden Banks          GC = Green Canyon
MC = Mississippi Canyon    ST = South Timbalier        VK = Viosca Knoll

Figures 25a and 25b illustrate the importance of the GOM to the Nation's energy supply. In 2005, the GOM supplied approximately 25 percent of the Nation's domestic oil and 16 percent of the Nation's domestic gas production. A significant portion of these volumes comes from deepwater. The slight reductions in the 2005 numbers result from the effects of Hurricanes Katrina and Rita.

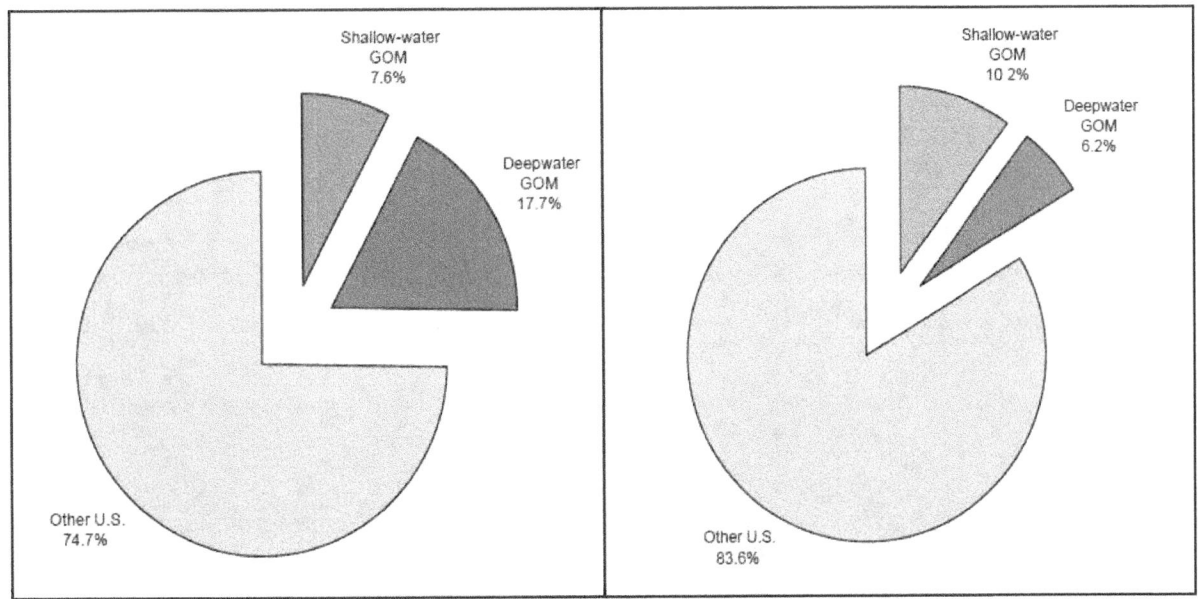

Figure 25a. OCS production as a percent of U.S. oil production.

Figure 25b. OCS production as a percent of U.S. gas production.

## PRODUCTION RATES

Numerous projects with royalty relief eligibility have come online in recent years. The impact of the DWRRA on deepwater production began to have its effect in 2002. Figure 26 uses a definition of 200 m (656 ft) for "deepwater" in order to compare the contribution from DWRRA leases where 200 m (656 ft) is the minimum water depth for which incentives are offered. In general, DWRRA oil reached its maximum contribution in 2004. Note the pre-DWRRA production refers to production from leases that have been approved to receive royalty relief but were issued before November 28, 1995.

A very similar comparison is seen in figure 27, where DWRRA gas is compared with total "deepwater" gas.

The declines of DWRRA production and total "deepwater" production in 2005 were hurricane related. Note the rapid rebound that continues to the end of the data on December 1, 2005. As of June 19, 2006, shut-in oil production is equivalent to approximately 12 percent of the daily oil production in the GOM and shut-in gas production is equivalent to approximately 9 percent of the daily gas production in the GOM (USDOI, MMS, 2006d). Appendix B contains data on the average annual GOM oil and gas production.

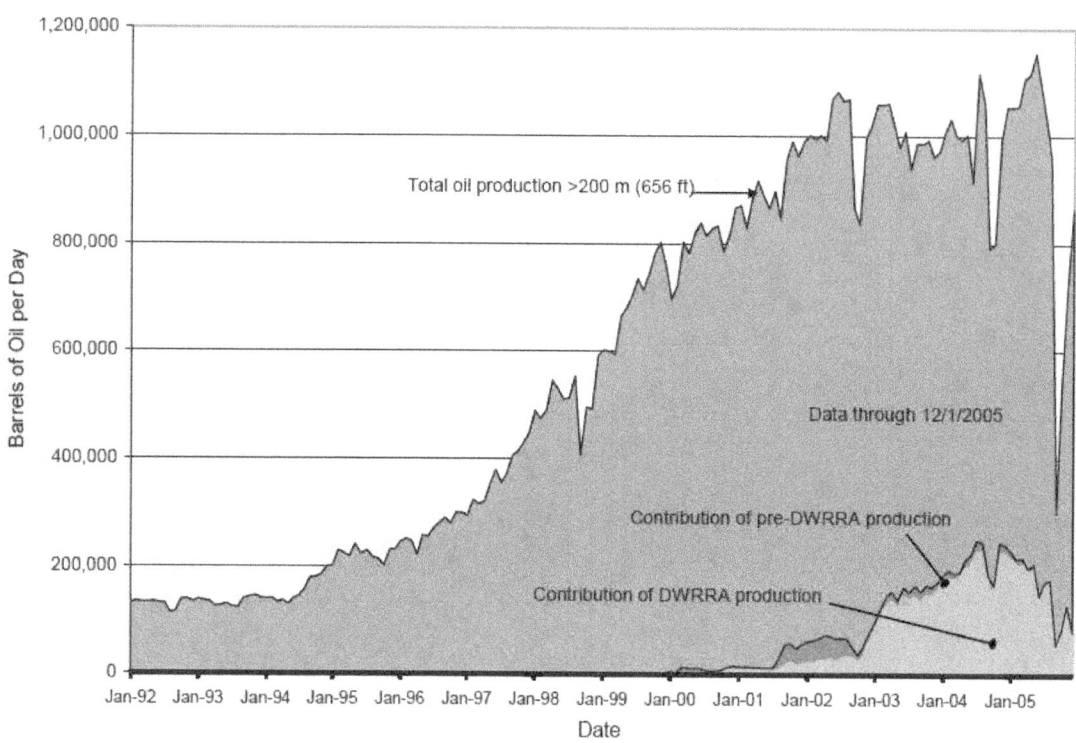

Figure 26. Contribution of DWRRA oil production to total oil production in water depths greater than 200 m (656 ft).

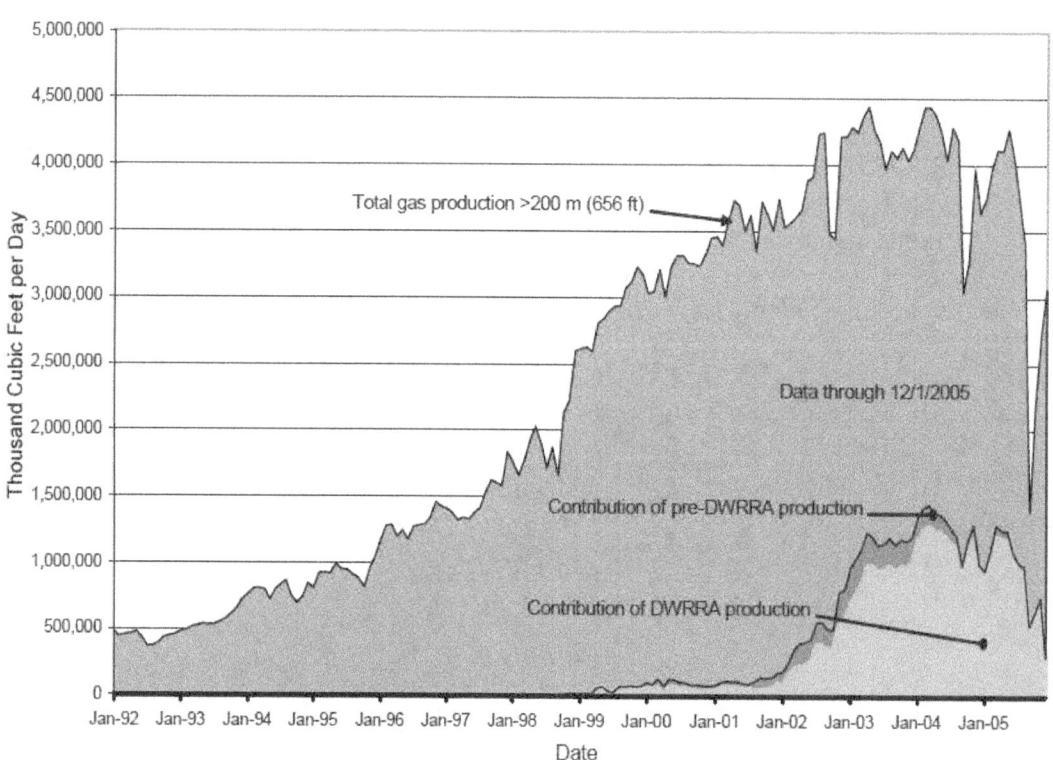

Figure 27. Contribution of DWRRA gas production to total gas production in water depths greater than 200 m (656 ft).

# SUMMARY AND CONCLUSIONS

Highlights from the 2007 deepwater report include the following.

- Twelve new deepwater discoveries were announced.

- Significant new discoveries and advances occurred in the Lower Tertiary trend.

- The Kaskida discovery was made.

- The Jack 2 well test was conducted.

- Great White and Chinook/Cascade developments were announced.

- Congress passed the Gulf of Mexico Energy Security Act of 2006 that

  - opens two new areas in the GOM for leasing,

  - places a leasing moratorium on some areas in the GOM, and

  - increases the distribution of offshore oil and gas revenues to coastal producing States.

- The royalty rate for deepwater leases was increased.

- New planning area/sale boundaries were announced.

- The spring 2007 Central GOM Lease Sale (Sale 205) is now tentatively scheduled for early October 2007. The MMS established a cutoff deadline of February 14, 2007, for inclusion of expired, relinquished, or terminated lease blocks for this sale.

- Increased deepwater tract availability is expected for future lease sales as a result of anticipated lease expirations, relinquishments, and terminations.

- The MMS approved 30 new technologies for use in the GOM.

- Nineteen of the top 20 producing blocks in the GOM for 2004-2005 were in deep water.

- Deepwater areas are responsible for approximately 70 percent of the oil and 40 percent of the gas produced in the GOM.

- Industry-announced discoveries in 2006 are estimated to total over 1.3 BBOE.

- Oil and gas prices averaged near $58.50 per barrel and $6.40 per Mcfg (USDOE, EIA, 2006).

The remainder of this section summarizes the development cycle and the challenges and rewards of the expanding deepwater frontier in the Gulf.

Figure 28 illustrates deepwater projects that began production in 2005-2006 and those expected to commence production in the next four years. The eastern concentration of projects expected to start production in 2007 is associated with Independence Hub.

41

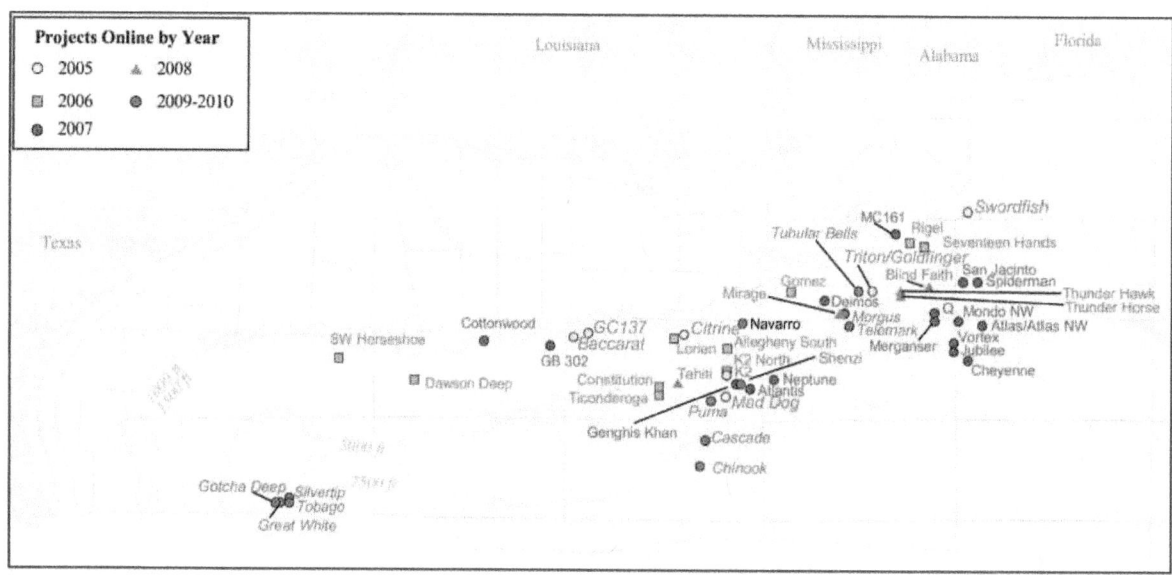

Figure 28. Deepwater projects starting production in 2005 and 2006 and those expected to begin production by yearend 2010.

In addition to the projects shown in figure 28, many more are likely to come online in the next few years. However, they are not shown in these figures because operators have not yet announced their plans. It is important to note that, in the next two years several very large developments will begin production. They include Thunder Horse at Mississippi Canyon Block 778, (250,000 barrels per day of oil and 197 million cubic feet per day of natural gas), Atlantis at Green Canyon Block 787 (200,000 barrels per day of oil and 180 million cubic feet per day of natural gas), and Tahiti at Green Canyon Block 640 (125,000 barrels per day of oil and 70 million cubic feet per day of natural gas).

## DEVELOPMENT CYCLE

Historic deepwater leasing activities do not show a strong relation to average oil or gas prices (figure 29). (Note that data in the last bar of figure 29 are reflective of 2006 information only.) There was considerable lease activity in the late 1980's despite low oil and gas prices. The very large increase in leasing activity beginning in 1996 was caused in part by the combination of

- DWRRA incentives,
- high production rates encountered at early deepwater fields, and
- several large early deepwater discoveries.

The sustained high levels of leasing activities in recent years are likely the result of a combination of continued exploration successes and high oil and gas prices.

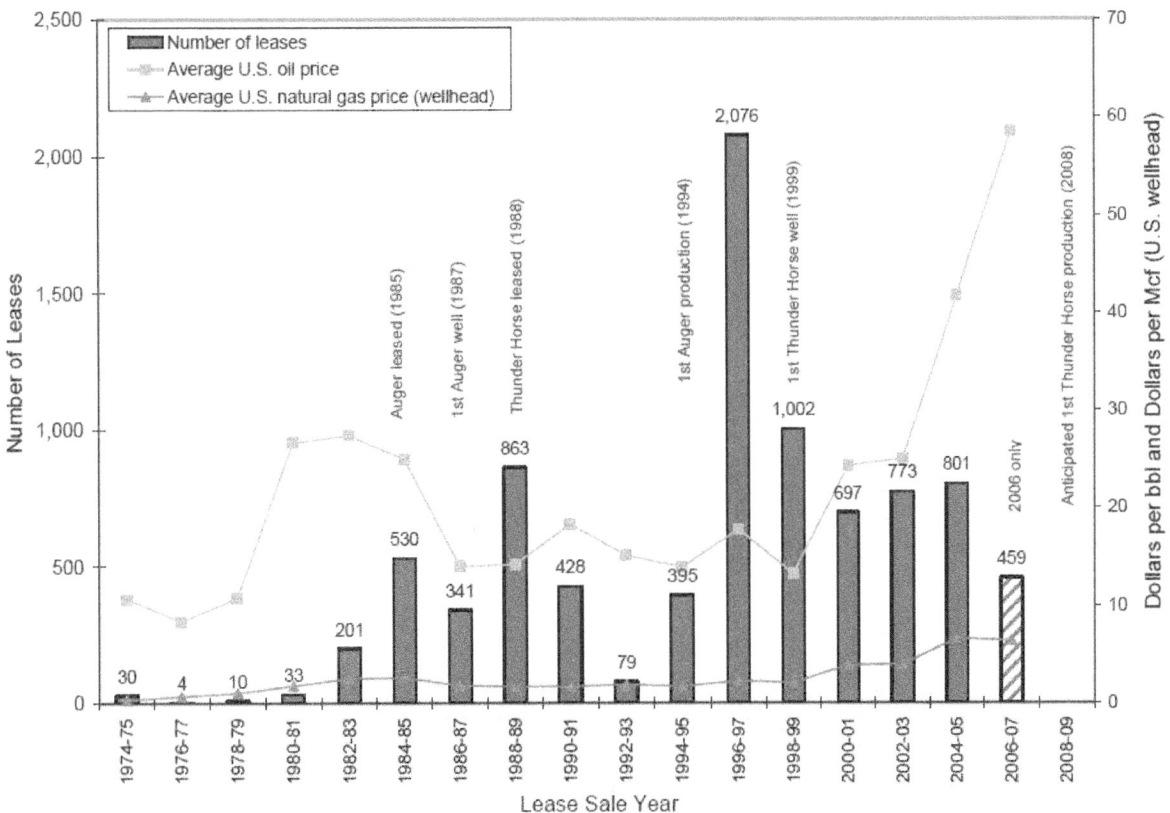

Figure 29. Deepwater lease activity and oil/natural gas prices.

There were approximately 3,000 leases issued during the record lease sales from 1996 to 1998. The available deepwater rig fleet is being challenged in its ability to evaluate the lease inventory. Other factors have also played a significant role in the industry's ability to evaluate their GOM lease inventory. These include alternative deepwater exploration and development targets throughout the world, capital limitations, rigs committed to development drilling on GOM deepwater discoveries, and limited qualified personnel. Many leases are now nearing the end of their primary terms, and operators are facing key decisions—which leases must be drilled prior to their lease expiration, which leases should be "farmed-out" to another company, or which leases should be relinquished without being "tested" (drilled).

Annotated also on figure 29 are key milestones at two important deepwater fields— Auger (Garden Banks Block 471) and Thunder Horse (Mississippi Canyon Block 778). The annotated milestones illustrate the lag time that can exist between the leasing of a prospect and first production. These long lag times are not unusual with complex deepwater developments.

Figure 30 does indicate that, as industry gains experience in the deepwater areas of the Gulf, the time between leasing and production is reduced. Developments near accessible infrastructure and the use of proven development technologies can also reduce the lag between leasing and production. However, as new discoveries move into dramatically deeper water depth, and with many new discoveries being far from existing infrastructure, an increase in lag time between leasing and production should be anticipated. Conditions such as high temperature and high pressure in wells will complicate drilling and development operations, resulting in longer lags as well.

The figure uses data from only productive deepwater leases and illustrates the lags between leasing and qualification and from qualification to first production. Operators sometimes announce discoveries to the public long before qualifying the lease as productive with MMS (and thereby granted field status). Note that, since deepwater leases are in effect for 8 or 10 years, the data are incomplete beyond 1996.

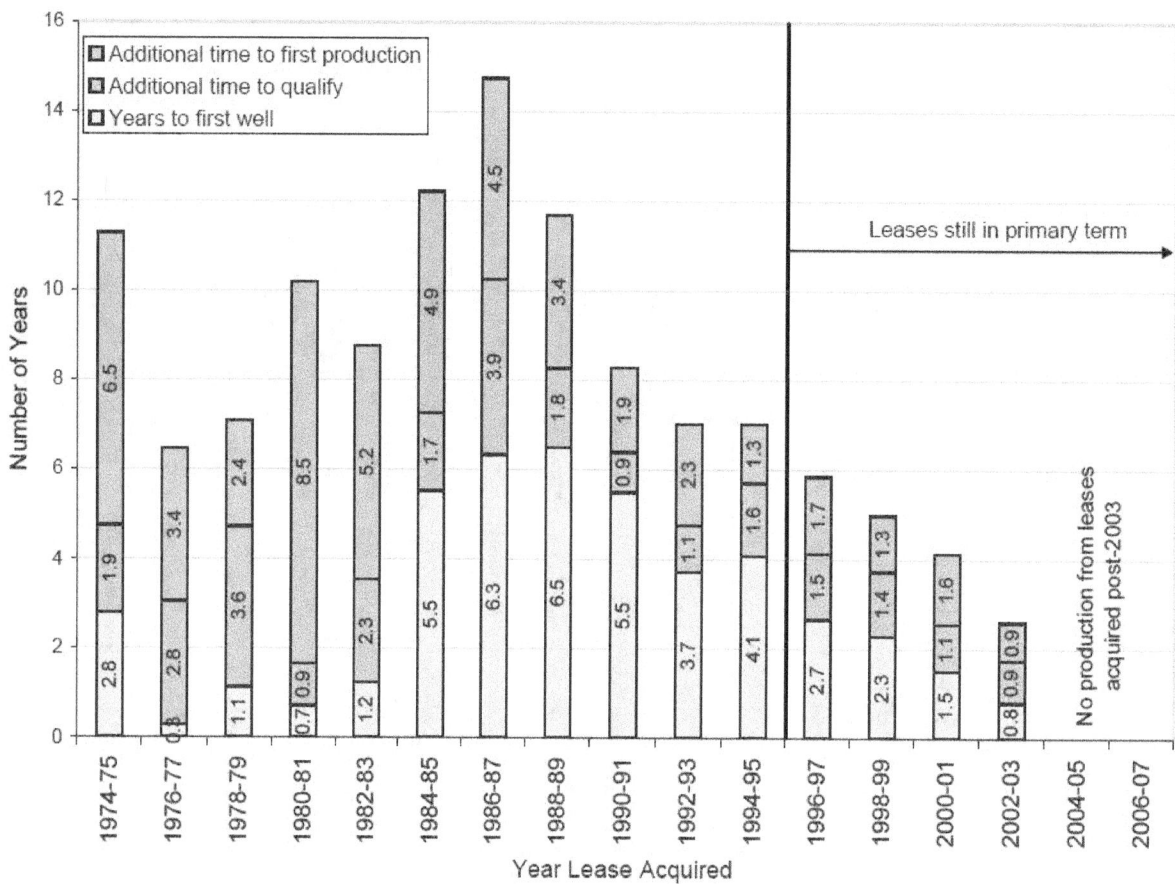

Figure 30. Average lag times from lease acquisition to first production for producing deepwater fields.

## EXPANDING FRONTIER

The future of deepwater GOM exploration and production remains very promising. Traditional deepwater mini-basin plays are far from mature, as several recent discoveries attest, and new deepwater plays near and even beyond the Sigsbee Escarpment, beneath thick salt canopies, and in lightly explored lower Tertiary reservoirs show that the deepwater GOM continues to be an expanding frontier. The 2000 Assessment (Lore et al., 2001) indicates that more than 50 billion recoverable BOE remains to be discovered. Since the start of 2000, new deepwater drilling has added over 6.5 BBOE to the Gulf.

The deepwater GOM continues to increase in its importance to the Nation's energy supply. The large number of active deepwater leases, the drilling of important new discoveries, the growing deepwater infrastructure, and the increasing deepwater production are all indicators of this maturing and yet still expanding frontier.

# CONTRIBUTING PERSONNEL

This report includes contributions from the following individuals:

Pat Adkins

Pat Bryars

Michael Dorner

Deborah Miller

Michelle Morin

Terry Rankin

Linda Wallace

# REFERENCES

Bascle, B.J., L.D. Nixon, and K.M. Ross. 2001. *Atlas of Gulf of Mexico Gas and Oil Reservoirs as of January 1, 1999.* U.S. Dept. of the Interior, Minerals Management Service, Gulf of Mexico OCS Region, New Orleans, LA. OCS Report MMS 2001-086, CD-ROM.

British Petroleum America Inc. (BP). 2006. BP Announces Gulf of Mexico Discovery. Press Release, August 31, 2006. Houston, TX. Internet website: http://www.bp.com/ genericarticle.do?categoryId=2012968&contentId=7022449.

Bush, G.W., President. 2007. Memorandum for the Secretary of the Interior. Modification of the June 12, 1998, Withdrawal of Certain Areas of the United States Outer Continental Shelf from Leasing Disposition. Office of the Press Secretary, January 9, 2007. Internet website: http://www.whitehouse.gov/news/releases/2007/01/ 20070109.html.

Chevron Corporation (Chevron). 2006. Chevron Announces Record Setting Well Test at Jack. Press Release, September 5, 2006. San Ramon, CA. Internet website: http:// www.chevron.com/news/press/2006/2006-09-05.asp.

Crawford, T.G., G.L. Burgess, C.J. Kinler, M.T. Prendergast, K.M. Ross, and N.K Shepard. 2006. *Estimated Oil and Gas Reserves, Gulf of Mexico, December 31, 2003.* U.S. Dept. of the Interior, Minerals Management Service, Gulf of Mexico OCS Region, New Orleans, LA. OCS Report MMS 2006-069. 48 pp.

Donohue, K., P. Hamilton, K. Leaman, R. Leben, M. Prater, D.R. Watts, and E. Waddell. 2006a. *Exploratory Study of Deepwater Currents in the Gulf of Mexico. Volume I: Executive Summary.* U.S. Dept. of the Interior, Minerals Management Service, Gulf of Mexico OCS Region, New Orleans, LA. OCS Study MMS 2006-073. 86 pp.

Donohue, K., P. Hamilton, K. Leaman, R. Leben, M. Prater, D.R. Watts, and E. Waddell. 2006b. *Exploratory Study of Deepwater Currents in the Gulf of Mexico. Volume II: Technical Report.* U.S. Dept. of the Interior, Minerals Management Service, Gulf of Mexico OCS Region, New Orleans, LA. OCS Study MMS 2006-074. 430 pp.

*Federal Register.* 2005. Oil and Gas and Sulphur Operations in the Outer Continental Shelf—Plans and Information; Final Rule. Tuesday, August 30, 2005. 70 FR 167, pp. 51477-51519.

*Federal Register.* 2006. Federal Outer Continental Shelf (OCS) Administrative Boundaries Extending from the Submerged Lands Act Boundary Seaward to the Limit of the United States Outer Continental Shelf. Tuesday, January 3, 2006. 71 FR 1, pp. 127-131.

*Federal Register.* 2007. Outer Continental Shelf (OCS), Eastern Gulf of Mexico (GOM), Oil and Gas Lease Sale 224 for 2008 (Call for Information and Nominations/Notice of Intent (Call/NOI) to Prepare a Supplemental Environmental Impact Statement (SEIS)). Wednesday, February 14, 2007. 72 FR 30, pp. 7070-7073.

French, L.S., E.G. Kazanis, L.C. Labiche, T.M. Montgomery, G.E. Richardson. 2005. *Deepwater Gulf of Mexico 2005: Interim Report of 2004 Highlights.* U.S. Dept. of the Interior, Minerals Management Service, Gulf of Mexico OCS Region, New Orleans, LA. OCS Report MMS 2005-023. 48 pp.

Hamilton, P., T.J. Berger, J.J. Singer, E. Waddell, J.H. Churchill, R.R. Leben, T.N. Lee, and W. Sturges. 2000. *DeSoto Canyon Eddy Intrusion Study: Final Report. Volume II: Technical Report.* U.S. Dept of the Interior, Minerals Management Service, Gulf of Mexico OCS Region, New Orleans, LA. OCS Study MMS 2000-80. 275 pp.

Hamilton, P., J.J. Singer, E. Waddell, and K. Donohue. 2003. *Deepwater Observations in the Northern Gulf of Mexico from In-Situ Current Meters and PIES, Volume II: Technical Report.* U.S. Dept. of the Interior, Minerals Management Service, Gulf of Mexico OCS Region, New Orleans, LA. OCS Report MMS 2003-049. 95 pp.

Kempthorne, D. 2007. Kempthorne May Offer Areas in the North Aleutian Basin, Central Gulf of Mexico for Leasing; Increase Royalty Rate for Offshore Oil and Gas Leases. Press Release, January 9, 2007. Washington, DC. Internet website: http://www.mms.gov/ooc/press/2007/pressdoi0109.htm

Lore, G.L., D.A. Marin, E.C. Batchelder, W.C. Courtwright, R.P. Desselles, Jr., and R.J. Klazynski. 2001. *2000 Assessment of Conventionally Recoverable Hydrocarbon Resources of the Gulf of Mexico and Atlantic Outer Continental Shelf as of January 1, 1999.* U.S. Dept. of the Interior, Minerals Management Service, Gulf of Mexico OCS Region, New Orleans, LA. OCS Report MMS 2001-087. 652 pp. CD-ROM only.

Mufson, S. 2006. U.S. Oil Reserves Get a Big Boost. washingtonpost.com, Wednesday, September 6, 2006. Washington, DC. Internet website: http://www.washingtonpost.com/wp-dyn/content/article/2006/09/05/AR2006090500275.html

Petroleo Brasileiro (Petrobras). 2006. US Regulators Approve Petrobras Plans to Bring First FPSO to the Gulf of Mexico. Press Release, December 11, 2006. Rio de Janeiro, Brazil. Internet website: http://www2.petrobras.com.br/publicacao/imagens/2885_chinook_e_cascade_final_ing.pdf.

Shell Offshore Inc. (Shell). 2006. Shell Announces Plans to Develop in the Ultra Deepwater of the Gulf of Mexico. News and Media Release, October, 26, 2006. Houston, TX. Internet website: http://www.shell.com/home/Framework?siteId=media-en&FC2=/media-en/html/iwgen/news_and_library/press_releases/2006/zzz_lhn.html&FC3=/media-en/html/iwgen/news_and_library/press_releases/2006/deepwater_gulf_mexico_26102006.html.

U.S. Dept. of Energy. Energy Information Administration. 2006. Monthly Energy Review, December 2006. Oil prices: http://tonto.eia.doe.gov/dnav/pet/hist/wtotusaw.htm. Natural gas prices: http://tonto.eia.doe.gov/dnav/ng/ng_pri_sum_dcu_nus_m.htm.

U.S. Dept. of the Interior, Minerals Management Service. 2000. Deepwater Gulf of Mexico OCS Currents. U.S. Dept. of the Interior, Minerals Management Service, Gulf of Mexico OCS Region, New Orleans, LA. MMS Safety Alert Notice No. 180.

U.S. Dept. of the Interior, Minerals Management Service. 2005. Deepwater Ocean Current Monitoring on Floating Facilities. U.S. Dept. of the Interior, Minerals Management Service, Gulf of Mexico OCS Region, New Orleans, LA. NTL 2005-G02.

U.S. Dept. of the Interior, Minerals Management Service. 2006a. The Lower Tertiary Trend. U.S. Dept. of the Interior, Minerals Management Service, Gulf of Mexico OCS Region, New Orleans, LA. *MMS Ocean Science*, November/December 2006. 3(6):4-7. Internet website: http://www.gomr.mms.gov/homepg/whatsnew/newsreal/2006/061010.pdf.

U.S. Dept. of the Interior, Minerals Management Service. 2006b. Information Requirements for Exploration Plans and Development Operations Coordination Documents. U.S. Dept. of the Interior, Minerals Management Service, Gulf of Mexico OCS Region, New Orleans, LA. NTL 2006-G14.

U.S. Dept. of the Interior, Minerals Management Service. 2006c. Guidance for Submitting Exploration Plans and Development Operations Coordination Documents. U.S. Dept. of the Interior, Minerals Management Service, Gulf of Mexico OCS Region, New Orleans, LA. NTL 2006-G15.

U.S. Dept. of the Interior, Minerals Management Service. 2006d. Hurricane Katrina/Hurricane Rita Evacuation and Production Shut-in Statistics Report as of Monday, June 19, 2006. Press Release #3528, June 21, 2006. U.S. Dept. of the Interior, Minerals Management Service, Gulf of Mexico OCS Region, New Orleans, LA. Internet website: http://www.mms.gov/ooc/press/2006/press0621.htm.

# APPENDICES

## APPENDIX A. DEVELOPMENT SYSTEMS OF PRODUCTIVE DEEPWATER GOM PROJECTS

| Year of First Production | Project Name[3] | Operator | Block | Water Depth (ft)[4] | System Type | DWRR[5] |
|---|---|---|---|---|---|---|
| 1979 | Cognac | Shell | MC 194 | 1,023 | Fixed Platform | |
| 1984 | Lena | ExxonMobil | MC 280 | 1,000 | Compliant Tower | |
| 1988[1] | GC 29 | Placid | GC 29 | 1,154 | Semisubmersible/ Subsea | |
| 1988[1] | GC 31 | Placid | GC 31 | 2,243 | Subsea | |
| 1989 | Bullwinkle | Shell | GC 65 | 1,353 | Fixed Platform | |
| 1989 | Jolliet | ConocoPhillips | GC 184 | 1,760 | TLP | |
| 1991 | Amberjack | BP | MC 109 | 1,100 | Fixed Platform | |
| 1992 | Alabaster | ExxonMobil | MC 485 | 1,438 | Subsea | |
| 1993[1] | Diamond | Kerr McGee | MC 445 | 2,095 | Subsea | |
| 1993 | Zinc | ExxonMobil | MC 354 | 1,478 | Subsea | |
| 1994 | Auger | Shell | GB 426 | 2,860 | TLP | |
| 1994 | Pompano/ Pompano II | BP | VK 989 | 1,290 | Fixed Platform/ Subsea | |
| 1994 | Tahoe/SE Tahoe | Shell | VK 783 | 1,500 | Subsea | |
| 1995[1] | Cooper | Newfield | GB 388 | 2,600 | Semisubmersible | |
| 1995[1] | Shasta | ChevronTexaco | GC 136 | 1,048 | Subsea | |
| 1995 | VK 862 | Walter | VK 862 | 1,043 | Subsea | |
| 1996 | Mars | Shell | MC 807 | 2,933 | TLP/Subsea | |
| 1996 | Popeye | Shell | GC 116 | 2,000 | Subsea | |
| 1996 | Rocky | Shell | GC 110 | 1,785 | Subsea | |
| 1997 | Mensa | Shell | MC 731 | 5,318 | Subsea | |
| 1997 | Neptune | Kerr McGee | VK 826 | 1,930 | Spar/Subsea | |
| 1997 | Ram-Powell | Shell | VK 956 | 3,216 | TLP | |
| 1997 | Troika | BP | GC 200 | 2,721 | Subsea | |
| 1998 | Arnold | Marathon | EW 963 | 1,800 | Subsea | |
| 1998 | Baldpate | Amerada Hess | GB 260 | 1,648 | Compliant Tower | |
| 1998 | Morpeth | Eni | EW 921 | 1,696 | TLP/Subsea | |
| 1998 | Oyster | Marathon | EW 917 | 1,195 | Subsea | |
| 1999 | Allegheny | Eni | GC 254 | 3,294 | TLP | |
| 1999 | Angus | Shell | GC 113 | 2,045 | Subsea | |
| 1999[1] | Dulcimer | Mariner | GB 367 | 1,120 | Subsea | Yes |
| 1999 | EW 1006 | Walter | EW 1006 | 1,884 | Subsea | |
| 1999 | Gemini | ChevronTexaco | MC 292 | 3,393 | Subsea | |
| 1999 | Genesis | ChevronTexaco | GC 205 | 2,590 | Spar | |

| Year of First Production | Project Name[3] | Operator | Block | Water Depth (ft)[4] | System Type | DWRR[5] |
|---|---|---|---|---|---|---|
| 1999 | Macaroni | Shell | GB 602 | 3,600 | Subsea | |
| 1999 | Penn State | Amerada Hess | GB 216 | 1,450 | Subsea | |
| 1999 | Pluto | Mariner | MC 674 | 2,828 | Subsea | Yes |
| 1999 | Ursa | Shell | MC 809 | 3,800 | TLP | |
| 1999 | Virgo | TotalFinaElf | VK 823 | 1,130 | Fixed Platform | Yes |
| 2000 | Black Widow | Mariner | EW 966 | 1,850 | Subsea | Yes |
| 2000 | Conger | Amerada Hess | GB 215 | 1,500 | Subsea | |
| 2000 | Diana | ExxonMobil | EB 945 | 4,500 | Subsea | |
| 2000 | Europa | Shell | MC 935 | 3,870 | Subsea | |
| 2000 | Hoover | ExxonMobil | AC 25 | 4,825 | Spar | |
| 2000 | King | Shell | MC 764 | 3,250 | Subsea | |
| 2000 | Marlin | BP | VK 915 | 3,236 | TLP | |
| 2000 | Northwestern | Amerada Hess | GB 200 | 1,736 | Subsea | Yes |
| 2000 | Petronius | ChevronTexaco | VK 786 | 1,753 | Compliant Tower | |
| 2001 | Brutus | Shell | GC 158 | 3,300 | TLP | |
| 2001 | Crosby | Shell | MC 899 | 4,400 | Subsea | |
| 2001 | Einset | Shell | VK 872 | 3,500 | Subsea | Yes |
| 2001 | EW 878 | Walter | EW 878 | 1,585 | Subsea | Yes |
| 2001 | Ladybug | ATP | GB 409 | 1,355 | Subsea | Yes |
| 2001 | Marshall | ExxonMobil | EB 949 | 4,376 | Subsea | |
| 2001[1] | MC 68 | Walter | MC 68 | 1,360 | Subsea | |
| 2001 | Mica | ExxonMobil | MC 211 | 4,580 | Subsea | |
| 2001 | Nile | BP | VK 914 | 3,535 | Subsea | |
| 2001 | Oregano | Shell | GB 559 | 3,400 | Subsea | |
| 2001 | Pilsner | Unocal | EB 205 | 1,108 | Subsea | Yes |
| 2001 | Prince | El Paso | EW 1003 | 1,500 | TLP | Yes |
| 2001 | Serrano | Shell | GB 516 | 3,153 | Subsea | |
| 2001 | Typhoon | ChevronTexaco | GC 237 | 2,679 | TLP | Yes |
| 2002 | Aconcagua | TotalFinaElf | MC 305 | 7,100 | Subsea | Yes |
| 2002 | Aspen | BP | GC 243 | 3,065 | Subsea | Yes |
| 2002 | North Boomvang[7] | Kerr McGee | EB 643 | 3,650 | Spar | Yes |
| 2003 | West Boomvang[7] | Kerr McGee | EB 642 | 3,678 | Subsea | Yes |
| 2003 | East Boomvang[7] | Kerr McGee | EB 688 | 3,795 | Subsea | Yes |
| 2002 | Madison | ExxonMobil | AC 24 | 4,856 | Subsea | |
| 2002 | King's Peak | BP | DC 133 | 6,845 | Subsea | Yes |
| 2002 | Lost Ark | Samedan | EB 421 | 2,960 | Subsea | Yes |
| 2002 | Nansen | Kerr McGee | EB 602 | 3,675 | Spar | Yes |
| 2002 | Navajo | Kerr McGee | EB 690 | 4,210 | Subsea | Yes |
| 2002 | Tulane | Amerada Hess | GB 158 | 1,054 | Subsea | Yes |
| 2002 | Manatee | Shell | GC 155 | 1,939 | Subsea | Yes |

| Year of First Production | Project Name[3] | Operator | Block | Water Depth (ft)[4] | System Type | DWRR[5] |
|---|---|---|---|---|---|---|
| 2002[1] | Sangria | Spinnaker | GC 177 | 1,487 | Subsea | Yes |
| 2002 | King Kong | Mariner | GC 472 | 3,980 | Subsea | Yes |
| 2002 | Yosemite | Mariner | GC 516 | 4,150 | Subsea | Yes |
| 2002 | Horn Mountain | BP | MC 127 | 5,400 | Spar | Yes |
| 2002[2] | Camden Hills | Marathon | MC 348 | 7,216 | Subsea | Yes |
| 2002 | Princess | Shell | MC 765 | 3,600 | Subsea | |
| 2002 | King | BP | MC 84 | 5,000 | Subsea | |
| 2003 | Falcon | Marubeni | EB 579 | 3,638 | Subsea | Yes |
| 2003 | Tomahawk | Marubeni | EB 623 | 3,412 | Subsea | Yes |
| 2003 | Habanero | Shell | GB 341 | 2,015 | Subsea | |
| 2003 | Durango[8] | Kerr McGee | GB 667 | 3,105 | Subsea | Yes |
| 2003 | Gunnison | Kerr McGee | GB 668 | 3,100 | Spar | Yes |
| 2003 | Dawson[8] | Kerr McGee | GB 669 | 3,152 | Subsea | Yes |
| 2003[2] | Boris | BHP | GC 282 | 2,378 | Subsea | Yes |
| 2003 | Matterhorn | TotalFinaElf | MC 243 | 2,850 | TLP | Yes |
| 2003[2] | Pardner | Anadarko | MC 401 | 1,139 | Subsea | Yes |
| 2003 | Zia | Devon | MC 496 | 1,804 | Subsea | |
| 2003 | Herschel/Na Kika | Shell | MC 520 | 6,739 | FPS/Subsea[6] | |
| 2003 | Fourier/Na Kika | Shell | MC 522 | 6,950 | FPS/Subsea[6] | |
| 2003 | North Medusa | Murphy | MC 538 | 2,223 | Subsea | Yes |
| 2003 | Medusa | Murphy | MC 582 | 2,223 | Spar | Yes |
| 2003 | East Anstey/ Na Kika | Shell | MC 607 | 6,590 | FPS/Subsea[6] | |
| 2004 | South Diana | ExxonMobil | AC 65 | 4,852 | Subsea | |
| 2004 | Hack Wilson | Kerr-McGee | EB 599 | 3,650 | Subsea | Yes |
| 2004[2] | Raptor | Marubeni | EB 668 | 3,710 | Subsea | Yes |
| 2004[2] | Harrier | Marubeni | EB 759 | 4,114 | Subsea | Yes |
| 2004 | Llano | Shell | GB 386 | 2,663 | Subsea | Yes |
| 2004 | Magnolia | ConocoPhillips | GB 783 | 4,674 | TLP | |
| 2004 | Red Hawk | Kerr-McGee | GB 877 | 5,334 | Spar | Yes |
| 2004 | Glider | Shell | GC 248 | 3,440 | Subsea | |
| 2004 | Front Runner | Murphy | GC 338 | 3,330 | Spar | Yes |
| 2004 | Marco Polo | Anadarko | GC 608 | 4,320 | TLP | Yes |
| 2004 | Holstein | BP | GC 645 | 4,344 | Spar | |
| 2004 | Kepler/Na Kika | BP | MC 383 | 5,759 | FPS/Subsea[6] | |
| 2004 | Ariel/Na Kika | BP | MC 429 | 6,274 | FPS/Subsea[6] | |
| 2004 | Coulomb/Na Kika | Shell | MC 657 | 7,591 | FPS/Subsea[6] | Yes |
| 2004 | MC 837 | Walter | MC 837 | 1,524 | Subsea | |
| 2005 | GC 137 | LLOG | GC 137 | 1,168 | Subsea | Yes |
| 2005 | Citrine | LLOG | GC 157 | 2,614 | Subsea | Yes |

| Year of First Production | Project Name[3] | Operator | Block | Water Depth (ft)[4] | System Type | DWRR[5] |
|---|---|---|---|---|---|---|
| 2005 | K2 | ENI | GC 562 | 4,006 | Subsea | |
| 2005 | Mad Dog | BP | GC 782 | 4,428 | Spar | |
| 2005 | Triton/Goldfinger | Dominion | MC 728 | 5,610 | Subsea | Yes |
| 2005 | Swordfish | Noble | VK 962 | 4,677 | Subsea | |
| 2005 | Baccarat | W and T Offshore | GC 178 | 1,404 | Subsea | Yes |
| 2006 | K2 North | Anadarko | GC 518 | 4,049 | Subsea | Yes |
| 2006 | Constitution | Kerr-McGee | GC 680 | 5,071 | Spar | Yes |
| 2006 | Ticonderoga | Kerr-McGee | GC 768 | 5,272 | Subsea | Yes |
| 2006 | Rigel | Dominion | MC 252 | 5,225 | Subsea | Yes |
| 2006 | Gomez | ATP | MC 711 | 3,098 | Semisubmersible | |
| 2006 | Seventeen Hands | Dominion | MC 299 | 5,881 | Subsea | Yes |
| 2006 | Lorien | Noble | GC 199 | 2,315 | Subsea | |
| 2006 | SW Horseshoe | Walter | EB 430 | 2,285 | Subsea | Yes |
| 2006 | Dawson Deep | Kerr McGee | GB 625 | 2,965 | Subsea | |
| 2006 | Allegheny South | ENI | GC 298 | 3,307 | Subsea | |
| 2007 | Genghis Khan | Anadarko | GC 652 | 4,300 | Subsea | |
| 2007 | Vortex | Anadarko | AT 261 | 8,344 | FPS/Subsea[9] | |
| 2007 | Jubilee | Anadarko | AT 349 | 8,825 | FPS/Subsea[9] | |
| 2007 | Spiderman | Anadarko | DC 621 | 8,087 | FPS/Subsea[9] | |
| 2007 | Merganser | Anadarko | AT 37 | 8,015 | FPS/Subsea[9] | |
| 2007 | Mondo NW | Anadarko | LL 1 | 8,340 | FPS/Subsea[9] | |
| 2007 | Cheyenne | Anadarko | LL 399 | 8,951 | FPS/Subsea[9] | |
| 2007 | Atlas/Atlas NW | Anadarko | LL 50 | 8,934 | FPS/Subsea[9] | |
| 2007 | Neptune | BHP | AT 575 | 6,220 | TLP | |
| 2007 | Atlantis | BP | GC 699 | 6,133 | Semisubmersible | |
| 2007 | San Jacinto | Dominion | DC 618 | 7,850 | FPS/Subsea[9] | |
| 2007 | Cottonwood | Petrobras | GB 244 | 2,130 | Subsea | |
| 2007 | Deimos | Shell | MC 806 | 3,106 | Subsea | |
| 2007 | Q | Spinnaker | MC 961 | 7,925 | FPS/Subsea[9] | |
| 2007 | GB 302 | Walter | GB 302 | 2,410 | Subsea | |
| 2007 | MC 161 | Walter | MC 161 | 2,924 | Subsea | |
| 2008 | Mirage | ATP | MC 941 | 3,927 | Subsea | |
| 2008 | Thunder Horse | BP | MC 778 | 6,089 | Semisubmersible | |
| 2008 | Tahiti | ChevronTexaco | GC 640 | 4,292 | Spar | |
| 2008 | Blind Faith | ChevronTexaco | MC 696 | 6,989 | Semisubmersible | |
| 2008 | Thunder Hawk | Murphy | MC 734 | 5,724 | Semisubmersible | |
| 2009 | Morgus | ATP | MC 942 | 3,960 | Subsea | |
| 2009 | Telemark | ATP | AT 63 | 4,385 | TLP | |
| 2009 | Navarro | ATP | GC 37 | 2,019 | | |

| Year of First Production | Project Name[3] | Operator | Block | Water Depth (ft)[4] | System Type | DWRR[5] |
|---|---|---|---|---|---|---|
| 2009 | Cascade | Petrobras | WR 206 | 8,143 | FPSO/Subsea | |
| 2009 | Chinook | Petrobras | WR 469 | 8,831 | FPSO/Subsea | |
| 2009 | Shenzi | BHP | GC 653 | 4,238 | TLP | |
| 2009 | Puma | BP | GC 823 | 4,129 | | |
| 2009 | Tubular Bells | BP | MC 725 | 4,334 | | |
| 2009 | Great White | Shell | AC 857 | 8,717 | Spar | |
| 2010 | Silvertip | Shell | AC 815 | 9,226 | Subsea | |
| 2010 | Tobago | Shell | AC 859 | 9,627 | Subsea | |
| 2010 | Gotcha Deep | TotalFinaElf | AC 856 | 7,815 | | |
| 2013 | Not releasable | | | | | |
| 2013 | Not releasable | | | | | |

[1] Off production – Lease(s) expired.

[2] Off production – Lease(s) active.

[3] Editions of this report prior to 2004 listed deepwater fields rather than projects. A block may be listed under more than one project name because of lease relinquishment, expiration, or termination and subsequent re-leasing. Some announced discoveries never reached the project stage and are listed under their prospect names.

[4] Water depths shown reflect depth at facility. If the project is subsea or undeveloped, water depth reflects depth of deepest well location in project.

[5] Indicates projects with one or more leases approved to receive Deep Water Royalty Relief.

[6] Na Kika FPS is located in Mississippi Canyon Block 474 in 6,340 ft (1,932 m) of water.

[7] 2004 Report referred to entire area as Boomvang.

[8] Included in 2004 Report with Gunnison.

[9] Independence Hub FPS is located in Mississippi Canyon Block 920 in 7,920 ft (2,414 m) of water.

| | | | |
|---|---|---|---|
| AC = Alaminos Canyon | AT = Atwater Valley | DC = DeSoto Canyon | EB = East Breaks |
| EW = Ewing Bank | GB = Garden Banks | GC = Green Canyon | LL = Lloyd Ridge |
| MC = Mississippi Canyon | VK = Viosca Knoll | WR = Walker Ridge | |

# APPENDIX B.  AVERAGE ANNUAL GOM OIL AND GAS PRODUCTION

| Year | Shallow-water Oil (MMbbl) | Deepwater Oil (MMbbl) | Total GOM Oil (MMbbl) | Shallow-water Gas (Bcf) | Deepwater Gas (Bcf) | Total GOM Gas (Bcf) |
|------|------|------|------|------|------|------|
| 1947 | 0 | 0 | 0 | 0 | 0 | 0 |
| 1948 | 0 | 0 | 0 | 0 | 0 | 0 |
| 1949 | 0 | 0 | 0 | 0 | 0 | 0 |
| 1950 | 0 | 0 | 0 | 0 | 0 | 0 |
| 1951 | 0 | 0 | 0 | 2 | 0 | 2 |
| 1952 | 1 | 0 | 1 | 19 | 0 | 19 |
| 1953 | 1 | 0 | 1 | 25 | 0 | 25 |
| 1954 | 2 | 0 | 2 | 60 | 0 | 60 |
| 1955 | 4 | 0 | 4 | 87 | 0 | 87 |
| 1956 | 7 | 0 | 7 | 91 | 0 | 91 |
| 1957 | 12 | 0 | 12 | 93 | 0 | 93 |
| 1958 | 20 | 0 | 20 | 144 | 0 | 144 |
| 1959 | 30 | 0 | 30 | 224 | 0 | 224 |
| 1960 | 41 | 0 | 41 | 281 | 0 | 281 |
| 1961 | 56 | 0 | 56 | 335 | 0 | 335 |
| 1962 | 77 | 0 | 77 | 451 | 0 | 451 |
| 1963 | 96 | 0 | 96 | 561 | 0 | 561 |
| 1964 | 111 | 0 | 111 | 645 | 0 | 645 |
| 1965 | 136 | 0 | 136 | 743 | 0 | 743 |
| 1966 | 175 | 0 | 175 | 992 | 0 | 992 |
| 1967 | 210 | 0 | 210 | 1285 | 0 | 1285 |
| 1968 | 254 | 0 | 254 | 1600 | 0 | 1600 |
| 1969 | 292 | 0 | 292 | 1950 | 0 | 1950 |
| 1970 | 329 | 0 | 329 | 2402 | 0 | 2402 |
| 1971 | 376 | 0 | 376 | 2729 | 0 | 2729 |
| 1972 | 373 | 0 | 373 | 3004 | 0 | 3004 |
| 1973 | 366 | 0 | 366 | 3312 | 0 | 3312 |
| 1974 | 338 | 0 | 338 | 3418 | 0 | 3418 |
| 1975 | 310 | 0 | 310 | 3427 | 0 | 3427 |
| 1976 | 301 | 0 | 301 | 3556 | 0 | 3556 |
| 1977 | 284 | 0 | 284 | 3767 | 0 | 3767 |
| 1978 | 276 | 0 | 276 | 4244 | 0 | 4244 |
| 1979 | 263 | 1 | 263 | 4671 | 0 | 4672 |
| 1980 | 260 | 5 | 265 | 4762 | 4 | 4766 |
| 1981 | 260 | 4 | 263 | 4886 | 3 | 4888 |
| 1982 | 273 | 13 | 286 | 4651 | 16 | 4666 |
| 1983 | 294 | 26 | 320 | 4034 | 41 | 4075 |
| 1984 | 330 | 25 | 355 | 4525 | 39 | 4564 |
| 1985 | 329 | 21 | 350 | 4024 | 34 | 4058 |

| Year | Shallow-water Oil (MMbbl) | Deepwater Oil (MMbbl) | Total GOM Oil (MMbbl) | Shallow-water Gas (Bcf) | Deepwater Gas (Bcf) | Total GOM Gas (Bcf) |
|------|---------------------------|-----------------------|-----------------------|-------------------------|---------------------|---------------------|
| 1986 | 336 | 19 | 356 | 4006 | 37 | 4043 |
| 1987 | 310 | 17 | 328 | 4481 | 44 | 4525 |
| 1988 | 288 | 13 | 301 | 4539 | 38 | 4577 |
| 1989 | 271 | 10 | 281 | 4604 | 32 | 4636 |
| 1990 | 262 | 12 | 275 | 4877 | 31 | 4908 |
| 1991 | 272 | 23 | 295 | 4649 | 58 | 4708 |
| 1992 | 268 | 37 | 305 | 4563 | 87 | 4651 |
| 1993 | 272 | 37 | 309 | 4536 | 120 | 4656 |
| 1994 | 272 | 42 | 314 | 4664 | 159 | 4824 |
| 1995 | 290 | 55 | 345 | 4598 | 181 | 4779 |
| 1996 | 297 | 72 | 369 | 4799 | 278 | 5077 |
| 1997 | 303 | 109 | 412 | 4764 | 382 | 5146 |
| 1998 | 285 | 159 | 444 | 4481 | 560 | 5042 |
| 1999 | 270 | 225 | 495 | 4212 | 846 | 5058 |
| 2000 | 252 | 271 | 523 | 3959 | 999 | 4958 |
| 2001 | 243 | 315 | 558 | 3877 | 1178 | 5054 |
| 2002 | 219 | 349 | 567 | 3237 | 1287 | 4524 |
| 2003 | 211 | 350 | 561 | 3001 | 1425 | 4426 |
| 2004 | 187 | 348 | 535 | 2604 | 1396 | 4000 |
| 2005 | 141 | 325 | 466 | 1954 | 1187 | 3142 |

# APPENDIX C. A MODIFICATION OF THE JUNE 12, 1998, WITHDRAWAL OF CERTAIN AREAS OF THE UNITED STATES OUTER CONTINENTAL SHELF FROM LEASING DISPOSITION

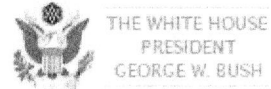

THE WHITE HOUSE
PRESIDENT
GEORGE W. BUSH

For Immediate Release
Office of the Press Secretary
January 9, 2007

## Memorandum for the Secretary of the Interior

SUBJECT: Modification of the June 12, 1998, Withdrawal of Certain Areas of the United States Outer Continental Shelf from Leasing Disposition

Under the authority vested in me as President of the United States, including section 12(a) of the Outer Continental Shelf Lands Act, 43 U.S.C. 1341(a), I hereby modify the first sentence of the withdrawal of June 12, 1998, of certain areas of the United States Outer Continental Shelf from leasing disposition to read as follows:

Under the authority granted in section 12(a) of the Outer Continental Shelf Lands Act, 43 U.S.C. 1341(a), I hereby withdraw from disposition by leasing through June 30, 2012, (1) those areas under moratoria pursuant to sections 104 and 106 of Public Law 109-54, and (2) those areas under moratoria pursuant to section 105 of Public Law 109 54, excluding that portion of the Central Gulf of Mexico planning area defined as the "181 South Area" in section 102(2) of title I ("Gulf of Mexico Energy Security") in Division C of Public Law 109 432, the Tax Relief and Health Care Act of 2006.

GEORGE W. BUSH

###

**Internet Website:**
http://www.whitehouse.gov/news/releases/2007/01/20070109.html

# APPENDIX D. SELECTED NTL's WITH 2006 EFFECTIVE DATES

Selected Notices to Lessees and Operators (NTL) of Federal Oil and Gas Leases in the Outer Continental Shelf (OCS) with Effective Dates in 2006.

| NTL Number | Title | Effective Date |
|---|---|---|
| 2006-G01 | Royalty Relief for Gulf of Mexico OCS Oil and Gas Leases with Facilities Damaged by Hurricane Katrina or Hurricane Rita | February 1, 2006 |
| 2006-G02 | Suspensions of Operations Based on Rig Delays, Lack of Rig Availability and Procurement of Long Lead Equipment | February 10, 2006 |
| 2006-G03 | Lease Term Extensions Pursuant to 30 CFR 250.180(e) Because of Hurricane Damage | February 10, 2006 |
| 2006-G07 | Revisions to the List of OCS Lease Blocks Requiring Archaeological Resource Surveys and Reports | March 16, 2006 |
| 2006-G12 | Ancillary Activities | July 3, 2006 |
| 2005-G20 (Addendum 1) | Damage Caused by Hurricanes Katrina and Rita (Addendum No. 1) | June 12, 2006 |
| 2006-G14 | Information Requirements for Exploration Plans and Development Operations Coordination Documents | July 12, 2006 |
| 2006-G15 | Guidance for Submitting Exploration Plans and Development Operations Coordination Documents | July 12, 2006 |
| 2006-G16 | Well Records Submittal (Updated) Elimination of Paper Copy Data Submittals | July 15, 2006 |
| 2006-N05 | Payment Method for New and Existing Cost Recovery Fees | September 1, 2006 |
| 2006-G17 | Conducting Platform Operations Before MMS Approval | September 7, 2006 |
| 2006-G19 | Hurricane and Tropical Storm Evacuation and Production Curtailment Statistics | October 25, 2006 |
| 2006-G20 | Mudline Suspension Wells: Dry Tree Tiebacks and Conversion to Subsea Wells | October 25, 2006 |
| 2006-G21 | Regional and Subregional Oil Spill Response Plans | October 26, 2006 |
| 2006-N07 | Participation in Post-Mortem Hurricane Initiatives | December 15, 2006 |
| 2006-N06 | Flaring and Venting Approvals | December 19, 2006 |

For a listing of all NTL's and electronic access to the full text of each, please go to the following MMS Internet website: www.gomr.mms.gov/homepg/regulate/regs/ntlltl.html.

# APPENDIX E. LEASE SALE RELATED INFORMATION

**Table E-1**
**Chronological Listing of GOM Lease Sales by Sale Location and Sale Date**

| Sale Number | Sale Location | Sale Date | Sale Number | Sale Location | Sale Date |
|---|---|---|---|---|---|
| 1 | LA[1] | 10/13/1954 | 51 | TX, LA | 12/19/1978 |
| 1S | LA | 10/13/1954 | 58 | GOM | 7/31/1979 |
| 2 | TX | 11/09/1954 | 58A | GOM | 11/27/1979 |
| 3 | TX, LA | 7/12/1955 | A62 | GOM | 9/30/1980 |
| 6 | LA[2] | 8/11/1959 | 62 | GOM | 11/18/1980 |
| 7 | TX, LA | 2/24/1960 | A66 | GOM | 7/21/1981 |
| 8 | LA[3] | 5/19/1960 | 66 | GOM | 10/20/1981 |
| 9 | LA | 3/13/1962 | 67 | GOM | 2/09/1982 |
| 10 | TX, LA | 3/16/1962 | 69 | GOM | 11/17/1982 |
| 11 | LA[2] | 10/09/1962 | 69A | GOM | 3/08/1983 |
| 12 | LA[2] | 4/28/1964 | 72 | CGOM | 5/25/1983 |
| 13 | SUL-TX[4] | 12/14/1965 | 74 | WGOM | 8/24/1983 |
| 14 | LA[2] | 3/29/1966 | 79 | EGOM | 1/05/1984 |
| 15 | LA[2] | 10/18/1966 | 81 | CGOM | 4/24/1984 |
| 16 | LA | 6/13/1967 | 84 | WGOM | 7/18/1984 |
| 17 | SA-LA[5] | 9/05/1967 | 98 | CGOM | 5/22/1985 |
| 18 | TX | 5/21/1968 | 102 | WGOM | 8/14/1985 |
| 19 | LA[2] | 11/19/1968 | 94 | EGOM | 12/18/1985 |
| 19A | LA[2] | 1/14/1969 | 104 | CGOM | 4/30/1986 |
| 20 | SUL-LA[6] | 5/13/1969 | 105 | WGOM | 8/27/1986 |
| 19B | LA[2] | 12/16/1969 | 110 | CGOM | 4/22/1987 |
| 21 | LA[2] | 7/21/1970 | 112 | WGOM | 8/12/1987 |
| 22 | LA | 12/15/1970 | SS | CGOM | 2/24/1988 |
| 23 | LA[2] | 11/04/1971 | 113 | CGOM | 3/30/1988 |
| 24 | LA | 9/12/1972 | 115 | WGOM | 8/31/1988 |
| 25 | LA | 12/19/1972 | 116 | EGOM | 11/16/1988 |
| 26 | TX, LA | 6/19/1973 | 118 | CGOM | 3/15/1989 |
| 32 | MAFLA[7] | 12/20/1973 | 122 | WGOM | 8/23/1989 |
| 33 | LA | 3/28/1974 | 123 | CGOM | 3/21/1990 |
| 34 | TX | 5/29/1974 | 125 | WGOM | 8/22/1990 |
| S1 | TX, LA | 7/30/1974 | 131 | CGOM | 3/27/1991 |
| 36 | LA | 10/16/1974 | 135 | WGOM | 8/21/1991 |
| 37 | TX | 2/04/1975 | 139 | CGOM | 5/13/1992 |
| 38 | TX, LA | 5/28/1975 | 141 | WGOM | 8/19/1992 |
| 38A | TX, LA | 7/29/1975 | 142 | CGOM | 3/24/1993 |
| 41 | GOM | 2/18/1976 | 143 | WGOM | 9/15/1993 |
| 44 | TX, LA | 11/16/1976 | 147 | CGOM | 3/30/1994 |
| 47 | GOM | 6/23/1977 | 150 | WGOM | 8/17/1994 |
| 45 | TX, LA | 4/25/1978 | 152 | CGOM | 5/10/1995 |
| 65 | GOM | 10/31/1978 | 155 | WGOM | 9/15/1995 |

63

| Sale Number | Sale Location | Sale Date | Sale Number | Sale Location | Sale Date |
|---|---|---|---|---|---|
| 157 | CGOM | 4/24/1996 | 181 | EGOM | 12/05/2001 |
| 161 | WGOM | 9/25/1996 | 182 | CGOM | 3/20/2002 |
| 166 | CGOM | 3/05/1997 | 184 | WGOM | 8/21/2002 |
| 168 | WGOM | 8/27/1997 | 185 | CGOM | 3/19/2003 |
| 169 | CGOM | 3/18/1998 | 187 | WGOM | 8/20/2003 |
| 171 | WGOM | 8/26/1998 | 189 | EGOM | 12/10/2003 |
| 172 | CGOM | 3/17/1999 | 190 | CGOM | 3/17/2004 |
| 174 | WGOM | 8/25/1999 | 192 | WGOM | 8/18/2004 |
| 175 | CGOM | 3/15/2000 | 194 | CGOM | 3/16/2005 |
| 177 | WGOM | 8/23/2000 | 196 | WGOM | 8/17/2005 |
| 178-1 | CGOM | 3/28/2001 | 197 | EGOM | 3/16/2005 |
| 178-2 | CGOM | 8/22/2001 | 198 | CGOM | 3/15/2006 |
| 180 | WGOM | 8/22/2001 | 200 | WGOM | 8/16/2006 |

[1] Sale 1 was an oil, gas, and sulfur lease sale offshore Louisiana.
[2] These were oil and gas drainage lease sales offshore Louisiana.
[3] Sale 8 was a salt lease sale offshore Louisiana.
[4] Sale 13 was a sulfur and salt lease sale offshore Texas.
[5] Sale 17 was a salt lease sale offshore Louisiana.
[6] Sale 20 was a sulfur and salt lease sale offshore Louisiana.
[7] Sale 32 was an oil and gas lease sale offshore Mississippi, Alabama, and Florida.
LA = oil and gas lease sale offshore Louisiana (unless otherwise footnoted)
TX = oil and gas lease sale offshore Texas
GOM = oil and gas lease sale in the Gulf of Mexico
CGOM = oil and gas lease sale in the Central Gulf of Mexico Planning Area
EGOM = oil and gas lease sale in the Eastern Gulf of Mexico Planning Area
WGOM = oil and gas lease sale in the Western Gulf of Mexico Planning Area

### Table E-2
### Lease Sale Schedule from the Proposed 5-Year Program for 2007-2012
(Until the Proposed 5-Year Program has been approved, the data
in the table must be considered tentative and subject to change.)

| Sale Number | Sale Location | Sale Date | Sale Number | Sale Location | Sale Date |
|---|---|---|---|---|---|
| 204 | WGOM | 2007 | 213 | CGOM | 2010 |
| 205 | CGOM | 2007 | 215 | WGOM | 2010 |
| 206 | CGOM | 2008 | 216 | CGOM | 2011 |
| 207 | WGOM | 2008 | 218 | WGOM | 2011 |
| 208 | CGOM | 2009 | 220 | Mid-Atlantic* | 2011 |
| 210 | WGOM | 2009 | 222 | CGOM | 2012 |

* This lease sale would only be held if the President chooses to modify the withdrawal in the area and Congress discontinues the annual appropriations moratorium in the Mid-Atlantic.

# NEWS RELEASE

FOR
RELEASE:

January 9, 2007

CONTACT: Gary Strasburg,    202-208-3985
         Shane Wolfe,      202-208-6416
         Nicolette Nye,    703-787-1011

## Kempthorne May Offer Areas in North Aleutian Basin, Central Gulf of Mexico for Leasing; Increases Royalty Rate for Offshore Oil and Gas Leases

**WASHINGTON**—Interior Secretary Dirk Kempthorne today announced that President George W. Bush has modified the leasing status of two areas in the Outer Continental Shelf in response to Congressional action and the requests of state leaders. In addition, Kempthorne announced that he has increased the royalty rate for most new offshore deepwater federal oil and gas leases to 16.7 percent (1/6th).

"Together, these actions will enhance America's energy security by improving opportunities for domestic energy production, and will also increase the revenues that the federal government collects from oil and gas companies on behalf of American taxpayers," Kempthorne said.

### New Areas

The areas were withdrawn from consideration for leasing through 2012 by President Bill Clinton in 1998. By modifying that Presidential withdrawal to remove these two areas, President Bush's action allows the Secretary of the Interior the option of offering these areas during the Minerals Management Service's next five-year OCS oil and gas leasing program (2007-2012).

"Both OCS areas—one in the North Aleutian Basin of Alaska, known as Bristol Bay, and the other in the Central Gulf of Mexico—would receive thorough environmental reviews," Kempthorne said. "There will be significant opportunities for study and public comment before any oil and gas development could take place in these areas."

Congress had imposed moratoria on oil and gas activities in the North Aleutian Basin from FY 1990 through FY 2003, but discontinued the yearly moratorium in FY 2004. In 2006, then-Alaska Governor Frank H. Murkowski and other local government and Native Alaskan leaders expressed support for modifying the Presidential withdrawal in the North Aleutian Basin.

Accordingly, the 2007-2012 OCS Oil and Gas Proposed Program, developed by Interior's Minerals Management Service (MMS), includes options for one or two lease sales in a small portion of the North Aleutian Basin—an area of about 5.6 million acres that was previously offered during Lease Sale 92 in 1988. The area would be subject to environmental reviews, including public comment, before any lease sale proceeds. There are no existing leases in the North Aleutian Basin.

The area in the Central Gulf of Mexico, referred to as the 181 South Area, comprises about 5.8 million acres in the Central Gulf of Mexico Planning Area, south of the 181 Area and west of the Military Mission Line and more than 125 miles from the coast of Florida. The 181 South Area was included in the 2007-2012 OCS Oil and Gas Proposed Program. In December 2006, Congress passed and President Bush signed the Gulf of Mexico Energy Security Act, which requires leasing in that area. MMS must conduct a detailed environmental review of the area before any leasing can occur there.

The 2007-2012 OCS Oil and Gas Proposed Final Program and Final Environmental Impact Statement are scheduled to be released in spring 2007.

### *Royalty Rate Increase*

The royalty rate increase to 16.7 (1/6$^{th}$ from the present 1/8$^{th}$) percent for new offshore (excluding Alaska) deepwater federal oil and gas leases will take effect with the first 2007 Gulf of Mexico lease sale scheduled for late August.

Most federal oil and gas is leased at a 12.5 percent royalty rate both onshore and offshore. The Outer Continental Shelf Lands Act (OCSLA) grants the Secretary of the Interior discretion to establish a higher royalty rate.

MMS estimates that the increased royalty rate of 16.7 percent for new deepwater offshore Gulf of Mexico leases will increase revenue from royalty payments by $4.5 billion over 20 years. MMS estimates that, by 2017, this increased revenue would offset any decline in bonus and rental revenues and any revenue losses from a decline in production. MMS estimates a decline of bonus and rental revenues at $820 million over 20 years and decline in production at 5 percent, or 110 million barrels of oil equivalent, over 20 years.

More information, including a fact sheet, maps of the areas and the President's memorandum is at http://www.mms.gov.

## TITLE I—GULF OF MEXICO ENERGY SECURITY

### SEC. 101. SHORT TITLE.

This title may be cited as the 'Gulf of Mexico Energy Security Act of 2006'.

### SEC. 102. DEFINITIONS.

In this title:

(1) 181 AREA—The term '181 Area' means the area identified in map 15, page 58, of the Proposed Final Outer Continental Shelf Oil and Gas Leasing Program for 1997-2002, dated August 1996, of the Minerals Management Service, available in the Office of the Director of the Minerals Management Service, excluding the area offered in OCS Lease Sale 181, held on December 5, 2001.

(2) 181 SOUTH AREA—The term '181 South Area' means any area—

(A) located—

(i)  south of the 181 Area;

(ii) west of the Military Mission Line; and

(iii)in the Central Planning Area;

(B) excluded from the Proposed Final Outer Continental Shelf Oil and Gas Leasing Program for 1997-2002, dated August 1996, of the Minerals Management Service; and

(C) included in the areas considered for oil and gas leasing, as identified in map 8, page 37 of the document entitled 'Draft Proposed Program Outer Continental Shelf Oil and Gas Leasing Program 2007-2012', dated February 2006 .

(3) BONUS OR ROYALTY CREDIT—The term 'bonus or royalty credit' means a legal instrument or other written documentation, or an entry in an account managed by the Secretary, that may be used in lieu of any other monetary payment for—

(A) a bonus bid for a lease on the outer Continental Shelf; or

(B) a royalty due on oil or gas production from any lease located on the outer Continental Shelf.

(4) CENTRAL PLANNING AREA—The term 'Central Planning Area' means the Central Gulf of Mexico Planning Area of the outer Continental Shelf, as designated in the document entitled 'Draft Proposed Program Outer Continental Shelf Oil and Gas Leasing Program 2007-2012', dated February 2006.

(5) EASTERN PLANNING AREA—The term 'Eastern Planning Area' means the Eastern Gulf of Mexico Planning Area of the outer Continental Shelf, as designated in the document entitled 'Draft Proposed Program Outer Continental Shelf Oil and Gas Leasing Program 2007-2012', dated February 2006.

(6) 2002-2007 PLANNING AREA—The term '2002-2007 planning area' means any area—

(A) located in—

(i) the Eastern Planning Area, as designated in the Proposed Final Outer Continental Shelf Oil and Gas Leasing Program 2002-2007, dated April 2002, of the Minerals Management Service;

(ii) the Central Planning Area, as designated in the Proposed Final Outer Continental Shelf Oil and Gas Leasing Program 2002-2007, dated April 2002, of the Minerals Management Service; or

(iii) the Western Planning Area, as designated in the Proposed Final Outer Continental Shelf Oil and Gas Leasing Program 2002-2007, dated April 2002, of the Minerals Management Service; and

(B) not located in—

(i) an area in which no funds may be expended to conduct offshore preleasing, leasing, and related activities under sections 104 through 106 of the Department of the Interior, Environment, and Related Agencies Appropriations Act, 2006 (Public Law 109-54; 119 Stat. 521) (as in effect on August 2, 2005);

(ii) an area withdrawn from leasing under the 'Memorandum on Withdrawal of Certain Areas of the United States Outer Continental Shelf from Leasing Disposition', from 34 Weekly Comp. Pres. Doc. 1111, dated June 12, 1998; or

(iii) the 181 Area or 181 South Area.

(7) GULF PRODUCING STATE—The term 'Gulf producing State' means each of the States of Alabama, Louisiana, Mississippi, and Texas.

(8) MILITARY MISSION LINE—The term 'Military Mission Line' means the north-south line at 86° 41′ W longitude

(9) QUALIFIED OUTER CONTINENTAL SHELF REVENUES—

(A) IN GENERAL—The term 'qualified outer Continental Shelf revenues' means—

(i) in the case of each of fiscal years 2007 through 2016, all rentals, royalties, bonus bids, and other sums due and payable to the United States from leases entered into on or after the date of enactment of this Act for—

(I) areas in the 181 Area located in the Eastern Planning Area; and

   (II) the 181 South Area; and

  (ii) in the case of fiscal year 2017 and each fiscal year thereafter, all rentals, royalties, bonus bids, and other sums due and payable to the United States received on or after October 1, 2016, from leases entered into on or after the date of enactment of this Act for—

   (I) the 181 Area;

   (II) the 181 South Area; and

   (III) the 2002-2007 planning area.

 (B) EXCLUSIONS—The term 'qualified outer Continental Shelf revenues' does not include—

  (i) revenues from the forfeiture of a bond or other surety securing obligations other than royalties, civil penalties, or royalties taken by the Secretary in-kind and not sold; or

  (ii) revenues generated from leases subject to section 8(g) of the Outer Continental Shelf Lands Act (43 U.S.C. 1337(g)).

(10) COASTAL POLITICAL SUBDIVISION—The term 'coastal political subdivision' means a political subdivision of a Gulf producing State any part of which political subdivision is—

 (A) within the coastal zone (as defined in section 304 of the Coastal Zone Management Act of 1972 (16 U.S.C. 1453)) of the Gulf producing State as of the date of enactment of this Act ; and

 (B) not more than 200 nautical miles from the geographic center of any leased tract.

(11) SECRETARY—The term 'Secretary' means the Secretary of the Interior.

# SEC. 103. OFFSHORE OIL AND GAS LEASING IN 181 AREA AND 181 SOUTH AREA OF GULF OF MEXICO.

 (a) 181 Area Lease Sale—Except as provided in section 104, the Secretary shall offer the 181 Area for oil and gas leasing pursuant to the Outer Continental Shelf Lands Act (43 U.S.C. 1331 et seq.) as soon as practicable, but not later than 1 year, after the date of enactment of this Act.

 (b) 181 South Area Lease Sale—The Secretary shall offer the 181 South Area for oil and gas leasing pursuant to the Outer Continental Shelf Lands Act (43 U.S.C. 1331 et seq.) as soon as practicable after the date of enactment of this Act .

 (c) Leasing Program—The 181 Area and 181 South Area shall be offered for lease under this section notwithstanding the omission of the 181 Area or the 181 South Area from any outer Continental Shelf leasing program under section 18 of the Outer Continental Shelf Lands Act (43 U.S.C. 1344).

(d) Conforming Amendment—Section 105 of the Department of the Interior, Environment, and Related Agencies Appropriations Act , 2006 (Public Law 109-54; 119 Stat. 522) is amended by inserting '(other than the 181 South Area (as defined in section 102 of the Gulf of Mexico Energy Security Act of 2006 ))' after 'lands located outside Sale 181'.

## SEC. 104. MORATORIUM ON OIL AND GAS LEASING IN CERTAIN AREAS OF GULF OF MEXICO.

(a) In General—Effective during the period beginning on the date of enactment of this Act and ending on June 30, 2022, the Secretary shall not offer for leasing, preleasing, or any related activity—

(1) any area east of the Military Mission Line in the Gulf of Mexico;

(2) any area in the Eastern Planning Area that is within 125 miles of the coastline of the State of Florida; or

(3) any area in the Central Planning Area that is—

(A) within—

(i) the 181 Area; and

(ii) 100 miles of the coastline of the State of Florida; or

(B)(i) outside the 181 Area;

(ii) east of the western edge of the Pensacola Official Protraction Diagram (UTM X coordinate 1,393,920 (NAD 27 feet)); and

(iii) within 100 miles of the coastline of the State of Florida.

(b) Military Mission Line—Notwithstanding subsection (a), the United States reserves the right to designate by and through the Secretary of Defense, with the approval of the President, national defense areas on the outer Continental Shelf pursuant to section 12(d) of the Outer Continental Shelf Lands Act (43 U.S.C. 1341(d)).

(c) Exchange of Certain Leases—

(1) IN GENERAL—The Secretary shall permit any person that, as of the date of enactment of this Act , has entered into an oil or gas lease with the Secretary in any area described in paragraph (2) or (3) of subsection (a) to exchange the lease for a bonus or royalty credit that may only be used in the Gulf of Mexico.

(2) VALUATION OF EXISTING LEASE—The amount of the bonus or royalty credit for a lease to be exchanged shall be equal to—

(A) the amount of the bonus bid; and

(B) any rental paid for the lease as of the date the lessee notifies the Secretary of the decision to exchange the lease.

(3) REVENUE DISTRIBUTION—No bonus or royalty credit may be used under this subsection in lieu of any payment due under, or to acquire any interest in, a lease subject to the revenue distribution provisions

of section 8(g) of the Outer Continental Shelf Lands Act (43 U.S.C. 1337(g)).

 (4) REGULATIONS—Not later than 1 year after the date of enactment of this Act, the Secretary shall promulgate regulations that shall provide a process for—

  (A) notification to the Secretary of a decision to exchange an eligible lease;

  (B) issuance of bonus or royalty credits in exchange for relinquishment of the existing lease;

  (C) transfer of the bonus or royalty credit to any other person; and

  (D) determining the proper allocation of bonus or royalty credits to each lease interest owner.

# SEC. 105. DISPOSITION OF QUALIFIED OUTER CONTINENTAL SHELF REVENUES FROM 181 AREA, 181 SOUTH AREA, AND 2002-2007 PLANNING AREAS OF GULF OF MEXICO.

 (a) In General—Notwithstanding section 9 of the Outer Continental Shelf Lands Act (43 U.S.C. 1338) and subject to the other provisions of this section, for each applicable fiscal year, the Secretary of the Treasury shall deposit—

  (1) 50 percent of qualified outer Continental Shelf revenues in the general fund of the Treasury; and

  (2) 50 percent of qualified outer Continental Shelf revenues in a special account in the Treasury from which the Secretary shall disburse—

   (A) 75 percent to Gulf producing States in accordance with subsection (b); and

   (B) 25 percent to provide financial assistance to States in accordance with section 6 of the Land and Water Conservation Fund Act of 1965 (16 U.S.C. 460l-8), which shall be considered income to the Land and Water Conservation Fund for purposes of section 2 of that Act (16 U.S.C. 460l-5).

 (b) Allocation Among Gulf Producing States and Coastal Political Subdivisions—

  (1) ALLOCATION AMONG GULF PRODUCING STATES FOR FISCAL YEARS 2007 THROUGH 2016—

   (A) IN GENERAL—Subject to subparagraph (B), effective for each of fiscal years 2007 through 2016, the amount made available under subsection (a)(2)(A) shall be allocated to each Gulf producing State in amounts (based on a formula established by the Secretary by regulation) that are inversely proportional to the respective distances between the point on the coastline of each Gulf producing State that is closest to the geographic center of the applicable leased tract and the geographic center of the leased tract.

(B) MINIMUM ALLOCATION—The amount allocated to a Gulf producing State each fiscal year under subparagraph (A) shall be at least 10 percent of the amounts available under subsection (a)(2)(A).

(2) ALLOCATION AMONG GULF PRODUCING STATES FOR FISCAL YEAR 2017 AND THEREAFTER—

(A) IN GENERAL—Subject to subparagraphs (B) and (C), effective for fiscal year 2017 and each fiscal year thereafter—

(i) the amount made available under subsection (a)(2)(A) from any lease entered into within the 181 Area or the 181 South Area shall be allocated to each Gulf producing State in amounts (based on a formula established by the Secretary by regulation) that are inversely proportional to the respective distances between the point on the coastline of each Gulf producing State that is closest to the geographic center of the applicable leased tract and the geographic center of the leased tract; and

(ii) the amount made available under subsection (a)(2)(A) from any lease entered into within the 2002-2007 planning area shall be allocated to each Gulf producing State in amounts that are inversely proportional to the respective distances between the point on the coastline of each Gulf producing State that is closest to the geographic center of each historical lease site and the geographic center of the historical lease site, as determined by the Secretary.

(B) MINIMUM ALLOCATION—The amount allocated to a Gulf producing State each fiscal year under subparagraph (A) shall be at least 10 percent of the amounts available under subsection (a)(2)(A).

(C) HISTORICAL LEASE SITES—

(i) IN GENERAL—Subject to clause (ii), for purposes of subparagraph (A)(ii), the historical lease sites in the 2002-2007 planning area shall include all leases entered into by the Secretary for an area in the Gulf of Mexico during the period beginning on October 1, 1982 (or an earlier date if practicable, as determined by the Secretary), and ending on December 31, 2015.

(ii) ADJUSTMENT—Effective January 1, 2022, and every 5 years thereafter, the ending date described in clause (i) shall be extended for an additional 5 calendar years.

(3) PAYMENTS TO COASTAL POLITICAL SUBDIVISIONS—

(A) IN GENERAL—The Secretary shall pay 20 percent of the allocable share of each Gulf producing State, as determined under paragraphs (1) and (2), to the coastal political subdivisions of the Gulf producing State.

(B) ALLOCATION—The amount paid by the Secretary to coastal political subdivisions shall be allocated to each coastal political subdivision in accordance with subparagraphs (B), (C); and (E) of section 31(b)(4) of the Outer Continental Shelf Lands Act (43 U.S.C. 1356a(b)(4)).

(c) Timing—The amounts required to be deposited under paragraph (2) of subsection (a) for the applicable fiscal year shall be made available in accordance with that paragraph during the fiscal year immediately following the applicable fiscal year.

(d) Authorized Uses—

(1) IN GENERAL—Subject to paragraph (2), each Gulf producing State and coastal political subdivision shall use all amounts received under subsection (b) in accordance with all applicable Federal and State laws, only for 1 or more of the following purposes:

(A) Projects and activities for the purposes of coastal protection, including conservation, coastal restoration, hurricane protection, and infrastructure directly affected by coastal wetland losses.

(B) Mitigation of damage to fish, wildlife, or natural resources.

(C) Implementation of a federally-approved marine, coastal, or comprehensive conservation management plan.

(D) Mitigation of the impact of outer Continental Shelf activities through the funding of onshore infrastructure projects.

(E) Planning assistance and the administrative costs of complying with this section.

(2) LIMITATION—Not more than 3 percent of amounts received by a Gulf producing State or coastal political subdivision under subsection (b) may be used for the purposes described in paragraph (1)(E).

(e) Administration—Amounts made available under subsection (a)(2) shall—

(1) be made available, without further appropriation, in accordance with this section;

(2) remain available until expended; and

(3) be in addition to any amounts appropriated under—

(A) the Outer Continental Shelf Lands Act (43 U.S.C. 1331 et seq.);

(B) the Land and Water Conservation Fund Act of 1965 (16 U.S.C. 460l-4 et seq.); or

(C) any other provision of law.

(f) Limitations on Amount of Distributed Qualified Outer Continental Shelf Revenues—

(1) IN GENERAL—Subject to paragraph (2), the total amount of qualified outer Continental Shelf revenues made available under subsection (a)(2) shall not exceed $500,000,000 for each of fiscal years 2016 through 2055.

(2) EXPENDITURES—For the purpose of paragraph (1), for each of fiscal years 2016 through 2055, expenditures under subsection (a)(2) shall be net of receipts from that fiscal year from any area in the 181 Area in the Eastern Planning Area and the 181 South Area.

(3) PRO RATA REDUCTIONS—If paragraph (1) limits the amount of qualified outer Continental Shelf revenue that would be paid under subparagraphs (A) and (B) of subsection (a)(2)—

(A) the Secretary shall reduce the amount of qualified outer Continental Shelf revenue provided to each recipient on a pro rata basis; and

(B) any remainder of the qualified outer Continental Shelf revenues shall revert to the general fund of the Treasury.

## The Department of the Interior Mission

As the Nation's principal conservation agency, the Department of the Interior has responsibility for most of our nationally owned public lands and natural resources.  This includes fostering sound use of our land and water resources; protecting our fish, wildlife, and biological diversity; preserving the environmental and cultural values of our national parks and historical places; and providing for the enjoyment of life through outdoor recreation. The Department assesses our energy and mineral resources and works to ensure that their development is in the best interests of all our people by encouraging stewardship and citizen participation in their care. The Department also has a major responsibility for American Indian reservation communities and for people who live in island territories under U.S. administration.

## The Minerals Management Service Mission

As a bureau of the Department of the Interior, the Minerals Management Service's (MMS) primary responsibilities are to manage the mineral resources located on the Nation's Outer Continental Shelf (OCS), collect revenue from the Federal OCS and onshore Federal and Indian lands, and distribute those revenues.

Moreover, in working to meet its responsibilities, the **Offshore Minerals Management Program** administers the OCS competitive leasing program and oversees the safe and environmentally sound exploration and production of our Nation's offshore natural gas, oil and other mineral resources.  The MMS **Minerals Revenue Management** meets its responsibilities by ensuring the efficient, timely and accurate collection and disbursement of revenue from mineral leasing and production due to Indian tribes and allottees, States and the U.S. Treasury.

The MMS strives to fulfill its responsibilities through the general guiding principles of:  (1) being responsive to the public's concerns and interests by maintaining a dialogue with all potentially affected parties and (2) carrying out its programs with an emphasis on working to enhance the quality of life for all Americans by lending MMS assistance and expertise to economic development and environmental protection.

www.ingramcontent.com/pod-product-compliance
Lightning Source LLC
Chambersburg PA
CBHW080321290526
45790CB00005B/2126